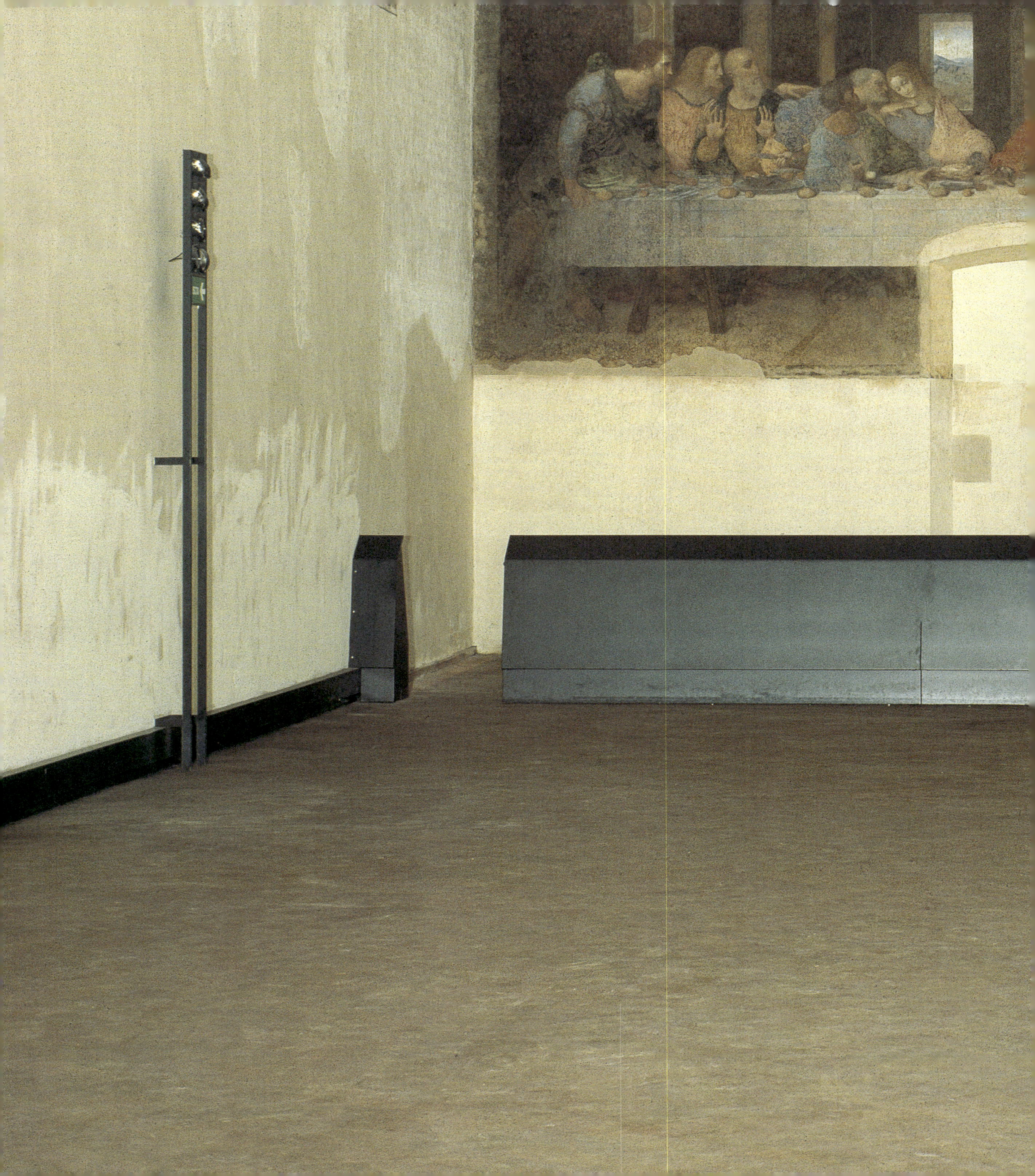

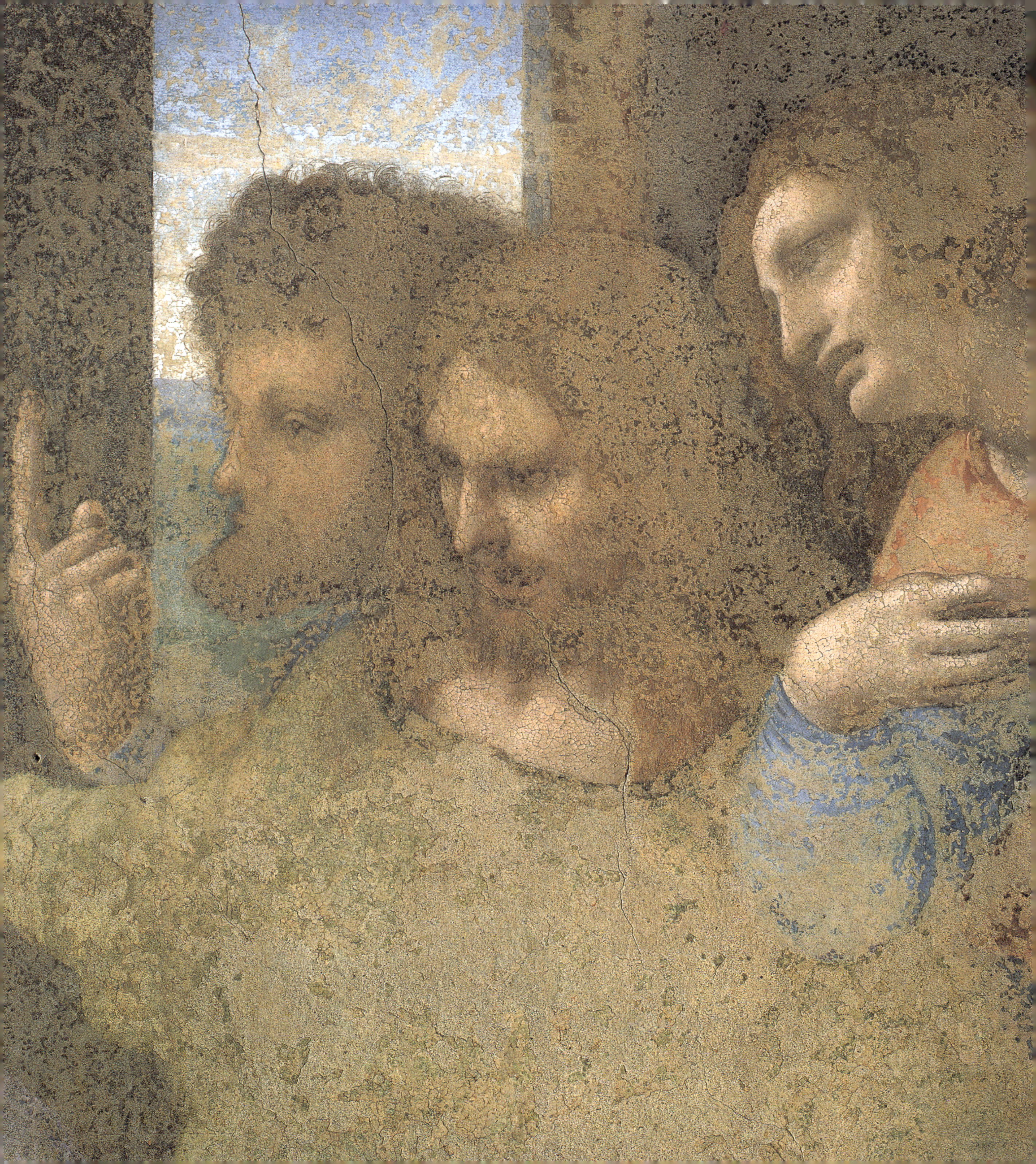

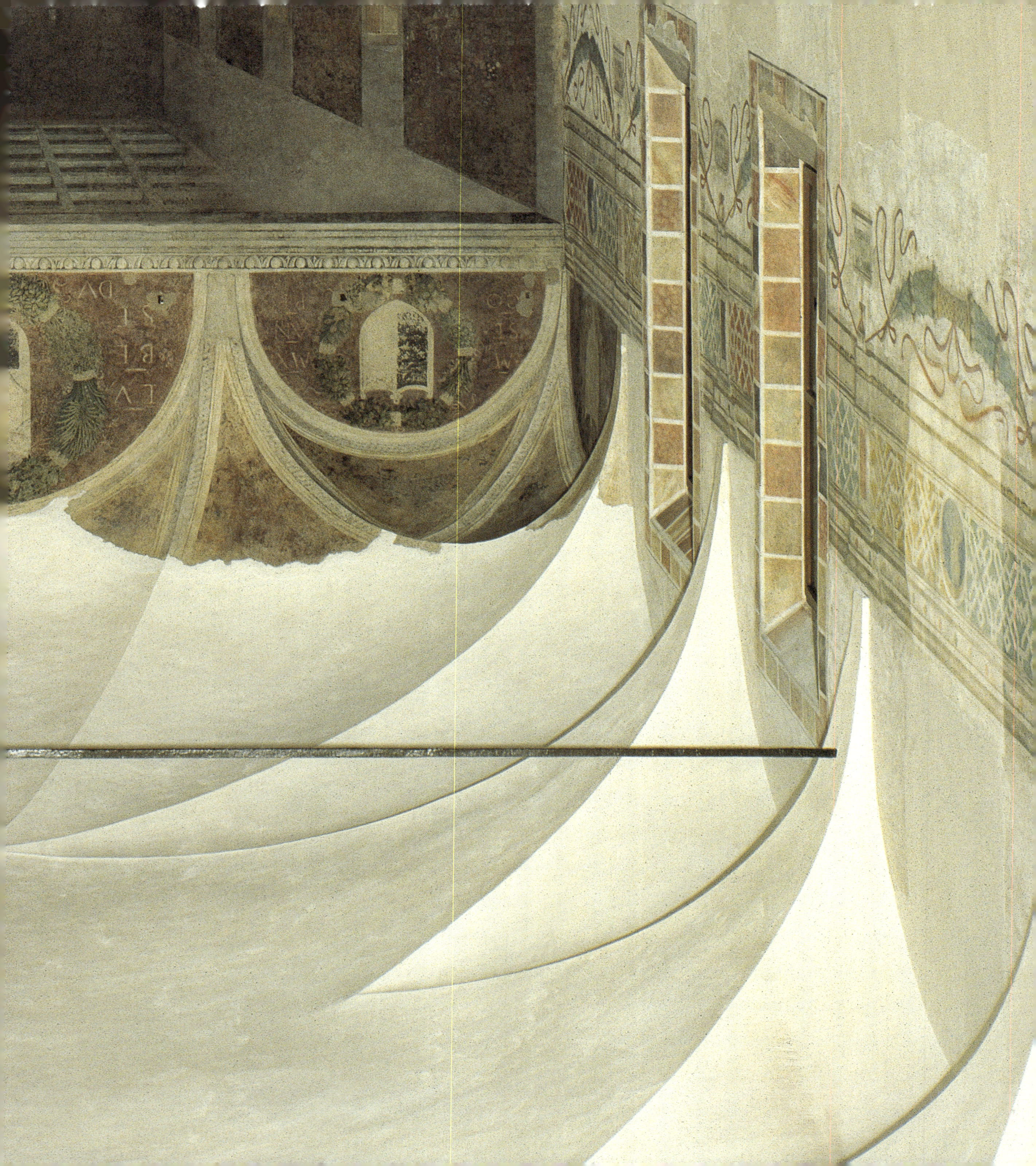

Leonardo Da Vinci — The Last Supper

a RizzoliQuadrifolio

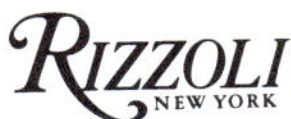

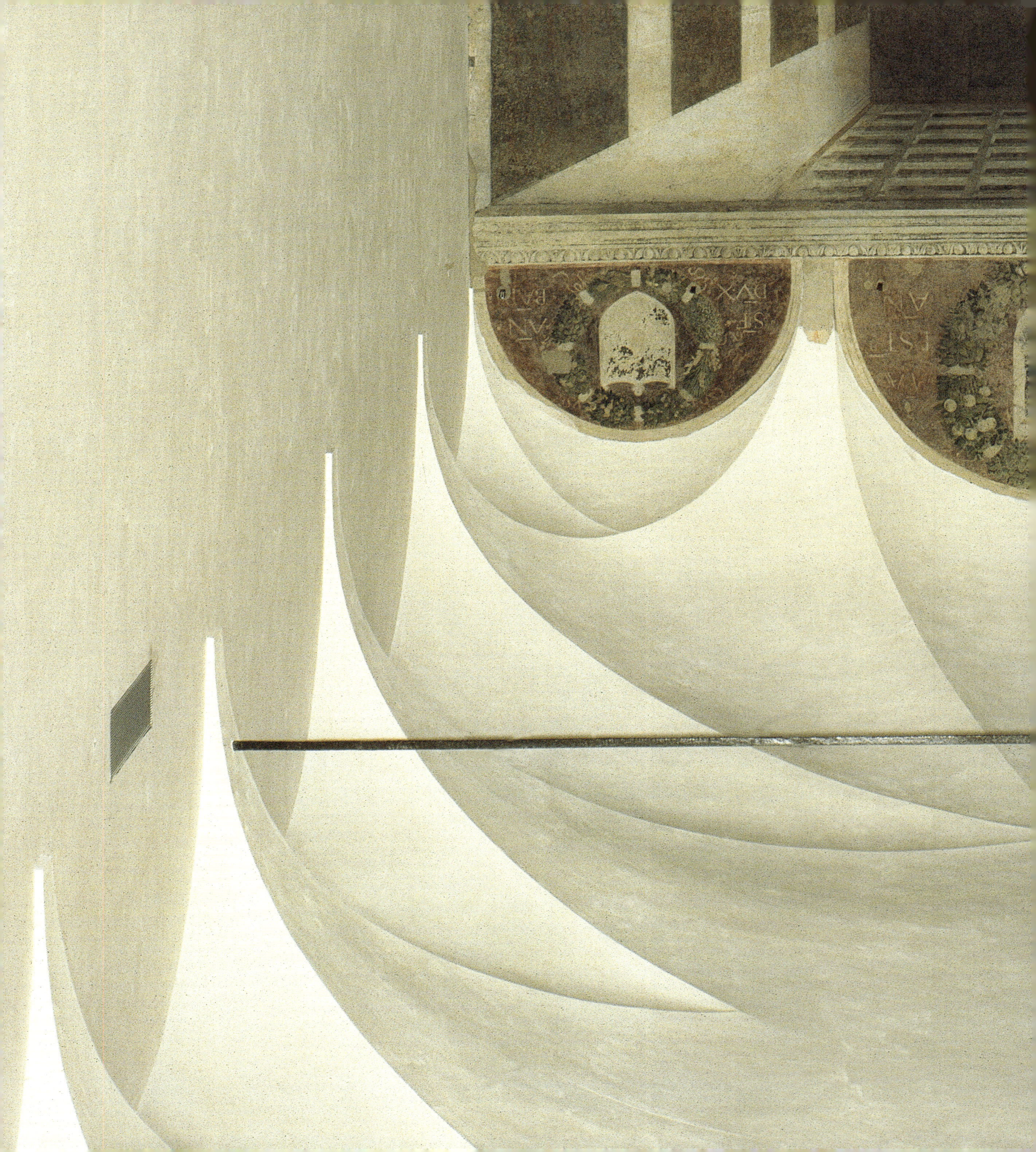

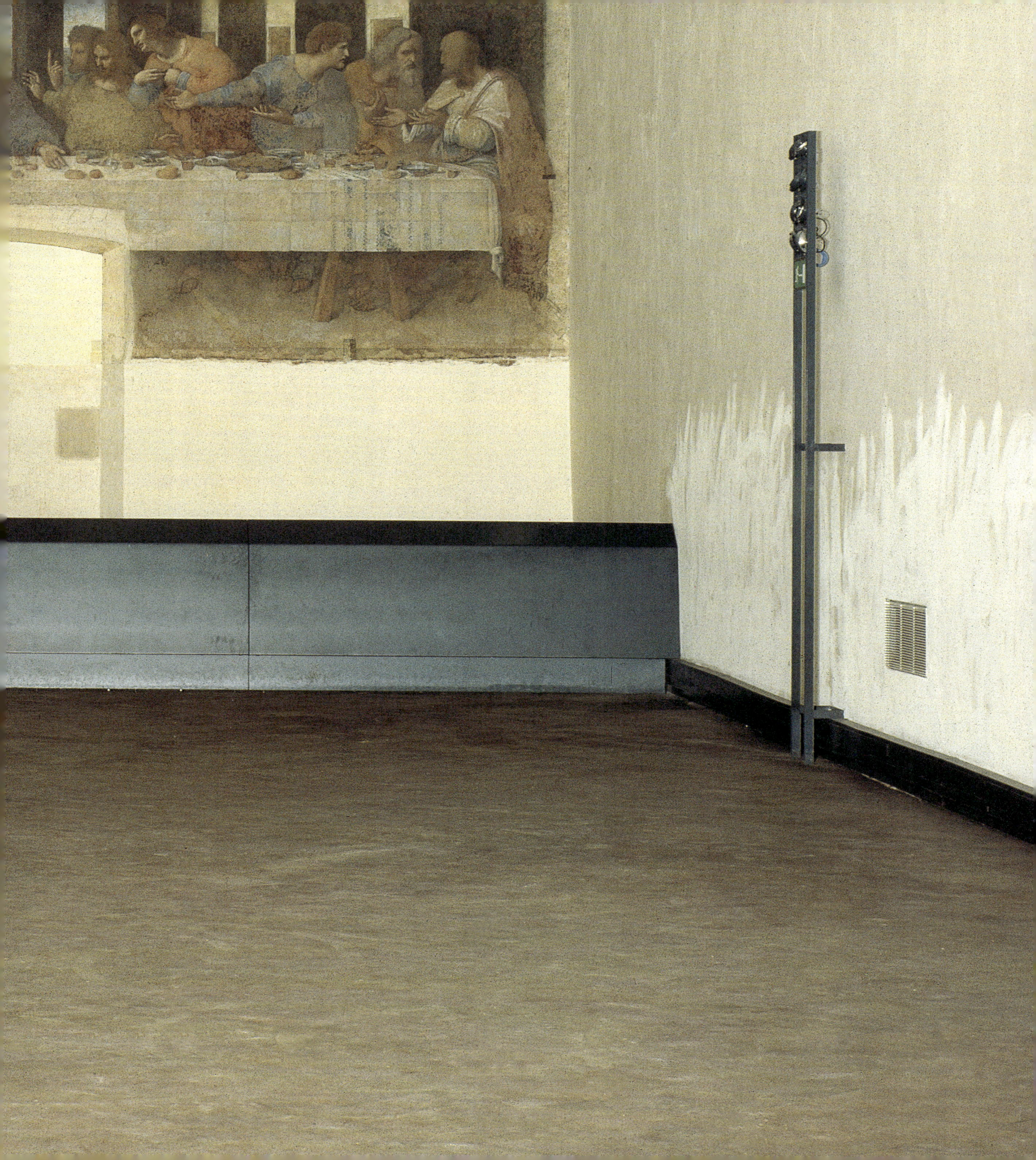

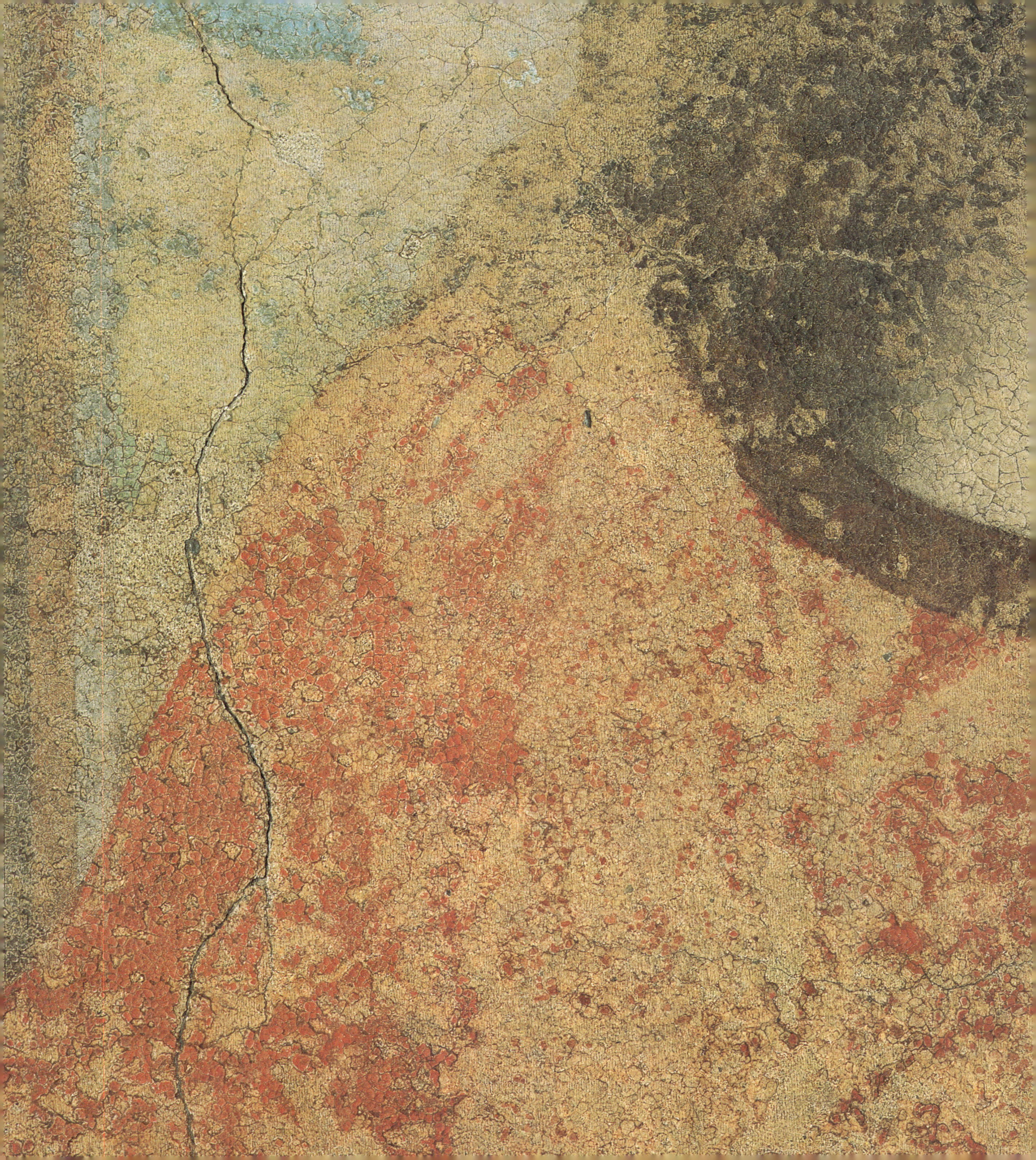

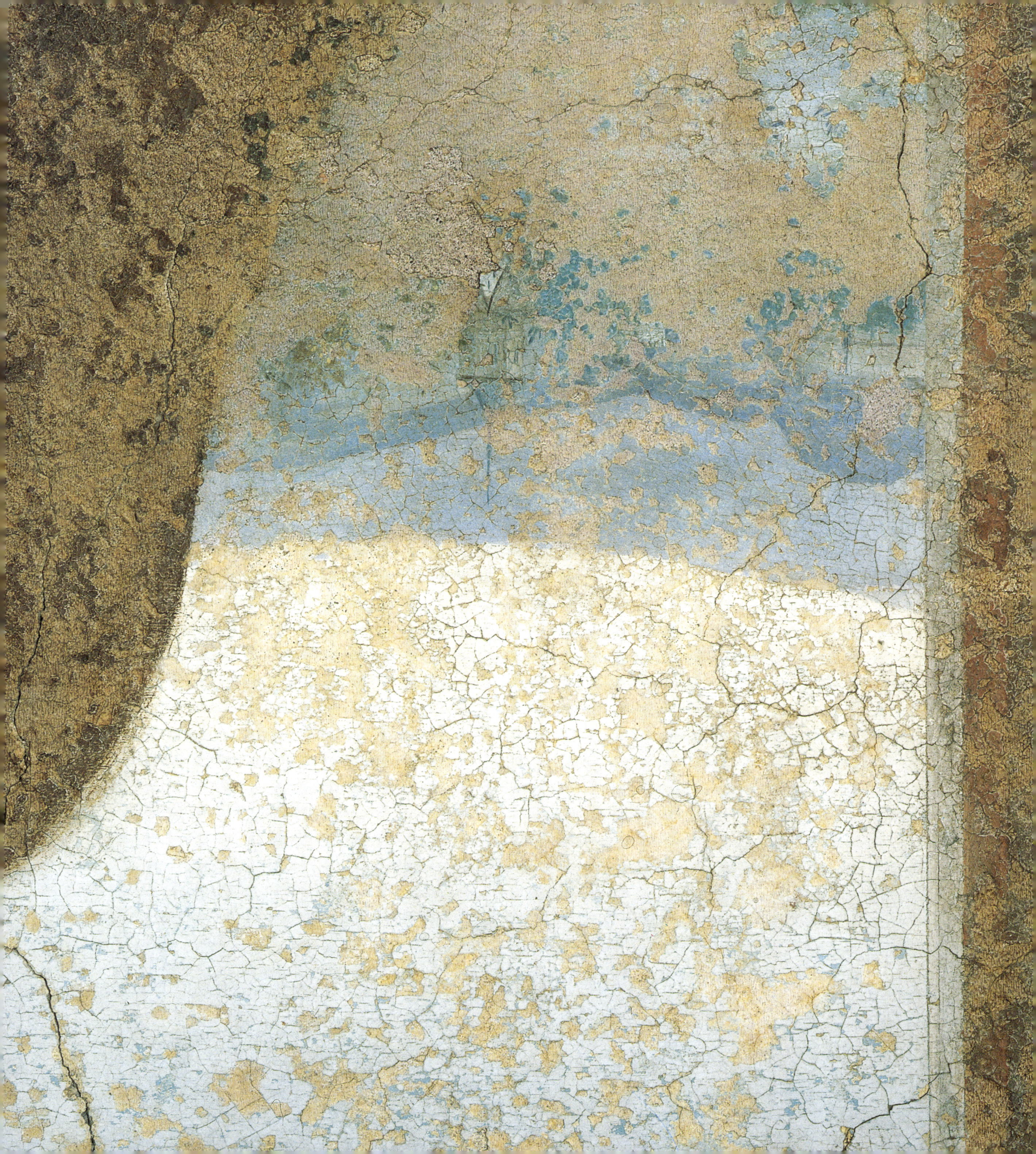

One of the most emblematic images of the Italian Renaissance, Leonardo da Vinci's *Last Supper* has always been admired, celebrated, and copied, notwithstanding its terrible state of preservation. The painting, already seriously compromised within a few years of its execution, deteriorated further over the centuries as a consequence of damage and repainting that eventually covered up much of Leonardo's original work. Leonardo's work, or what remains of it, has only recently been brought to light by the latest restoration and conservation, which took place over a period of twenty years.

Unfortunately, there are no surviving documents in the archives relating to the commission and payments for the picture, painted by Leonardo on one of the shorter walls of the refectory of the monastery annexed to the church of Santa Maria delle Grazie in Milan. However, an approximate chronology of the work can be deduced from a number of contemporary accounts that have come down to us. In a letter sent on June 29, 1497, Duke Ludovico Sforza of Milan, better known as Ludovico il Moro, requested that his secretary Marchesino Stanga urge Leonardo to finish the work he had started. It must have been completed by February 8 of the following year, as it was described by the mathematician Luca Pacioli in the dedicatory letter, addressed to Ludovico il Moro, of his treatise *De Divina Proportione*, which was written on this date.

Several suppositions can be made on the basis of this evidence: first, that the person who commissioned the *Last Supper* was the duke of Milan himself, something that we can also deduce from the presence of the latter's charge in the central lunette above the painting, flanked in turn by four more lunettes (two on the same wall and two on the side walls) bearing the Sforza coat of arms. It is also known that Leonardo had spent much of his first visit to Milan (from 1492 to 1499) in the duke's employ, after offering his services to him in the celebrated letter of introduction which already refers to the colossal, never-completed undertaking of the bronze equestrian monument to Francesco Sforza, one of the most ambitious forms of dynastic celebration ever conceived.

Another assumption that can be deduced from the sources is that Leonardo worked on the *Last Supper* for several years, perhaps from 1495 or even earlier, as is suggested by a number of preparatory drawings that can be dated to an even earlier date. In this respect the question of Leonardo's slow and irregular manner of working also has to be taken into consideration. Direct testimony of this, and in connection with the *Last Supper* itself, was provided by the short-story writer Matteo Bandello in 1498. In fact Bandello claimed that the artist had only given sporadic attention to the work—sometimes for whole days at a time, without "ever putting down his brush, but forgetting to eat and drink," sometimes simply looking at the painting in progress for "one or two hours a day" and at others, "as the whim or fancy took him. . . picking up the brush, and giving one or two strokes to one of the figures and then immediately leaving and going somewhere else." It goes without saying that such an approach to the work was totally incompatible with the technique of *buon fresco*, which would have guaranteed the durability of the painting over a long period of time, but which, as is well known, requires speed of execution and leaves no scope for significant alterations in the course of the work.

In the *Last Supper*, on the contrary, Leonardo experimented with a "dry" technique of mural painting, using a mixture of tempera and oil on a double layer of plaster. Such a procedure was undoubtedly better suited both to his slow and thoughtful method of working and to the attainment of a fuller range of colors, richer in subtle modulations of light and shade; however, it proved detrimental to the preservation of the painting, soon causing it to embark on a long and inexorable process of deterioration.

In spite of this, the *Last Supper* remains an exemplary product of Leonardo's genius, in which the great master's artistic and scientific interests are organically fused. In fact he saw scientific observation and artistic production as two distinct phases in a single process aimed at understanding humanity and the universe, viewed in terms of the analogical model of microcosm and macrocosm and conceived as creations of God, the "Prime Mover," who brought them into existence. Leonardo's handling of the scene, though still influenced in its iconography by precedents from the Florentine tradition, was actually totally new and original. The episode from the New Testament, the moment when Jesus reveals that he will be betrayed by one of the apostles, is represented by the artist as a natural phenomenon involving movements of both the spirit and the body. The words pronounced by Jesus provoke a reaction of dismay in those present that Leonardo conveys through an incredible variety of gestures, attitudes, and expressions, creating a dynamic, interconnected, and rationally composed ensemble with the figure of Christ at its center. The latter, motionless in resignation to his fate, is at the same time the driving force of a movement that spreads through the apostles, divided into groups of three. It has been pointed out that this compositional structure is reminiscent of some of Leonardo's writings on the diffusion of mechanical motion, in particular the one relating to his observation of the phenomenon of the concentric ripples that are formed in a pool of water around the point into which a stone has been thrown.

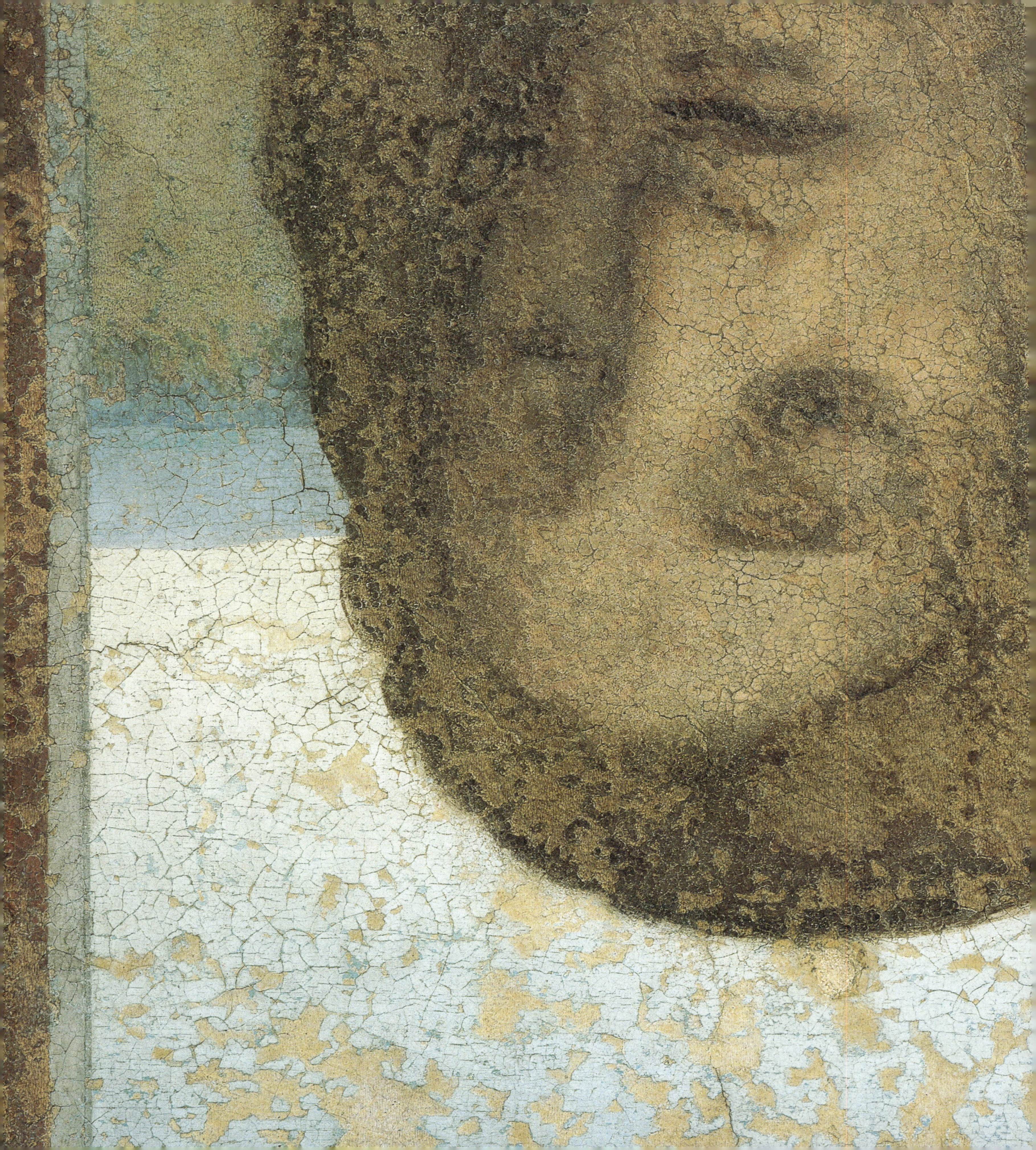

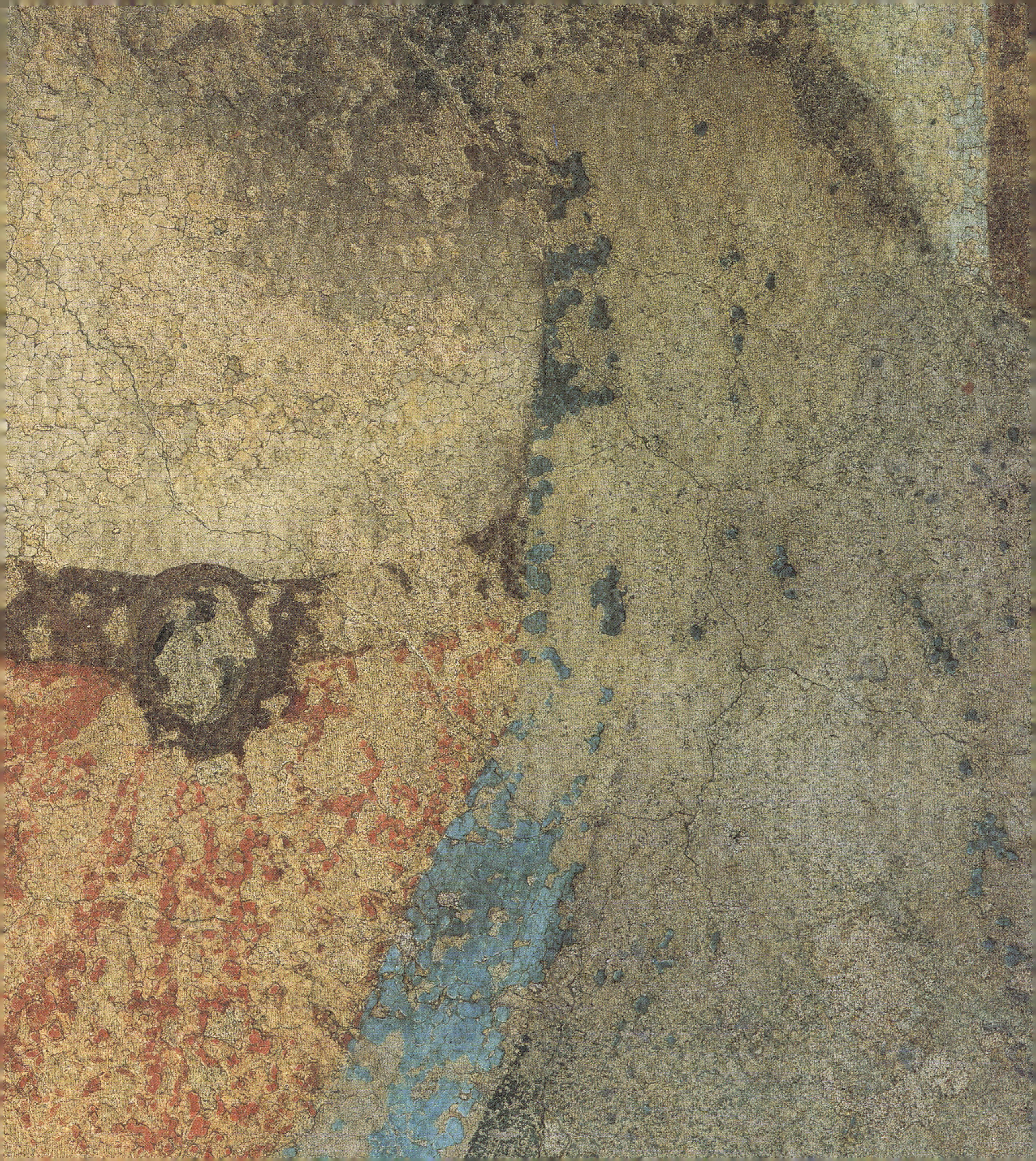

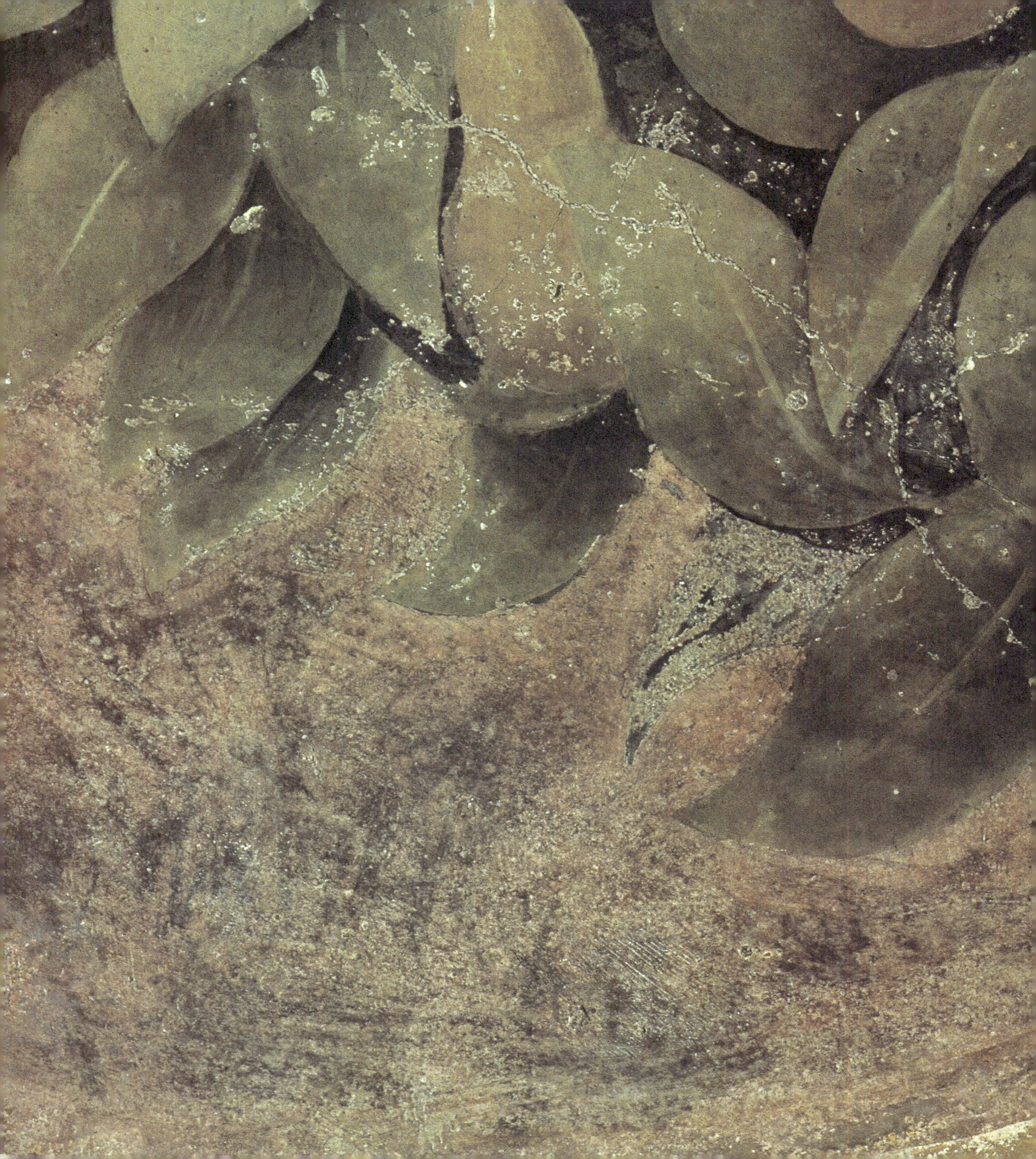

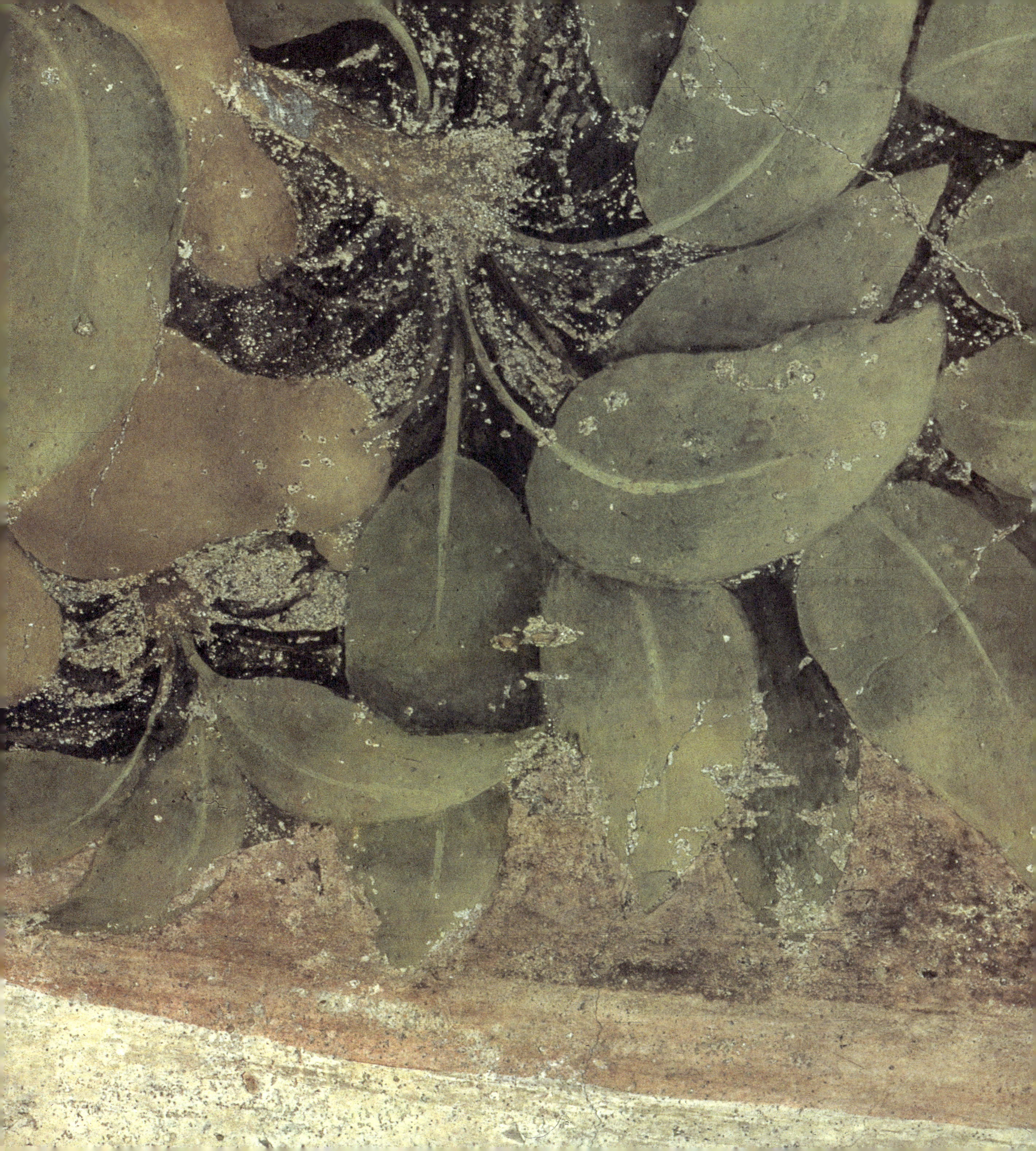

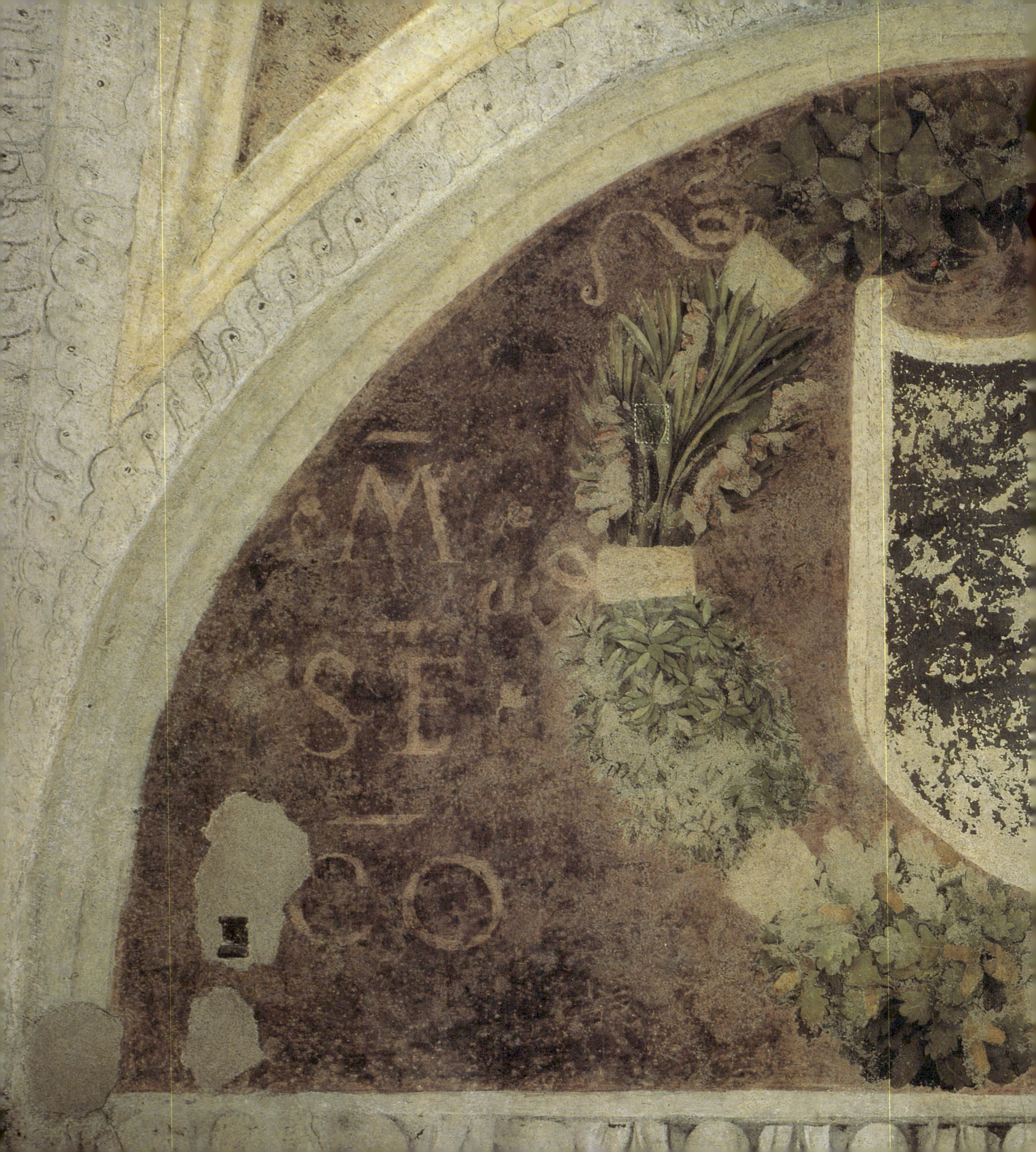
M
SE
CO

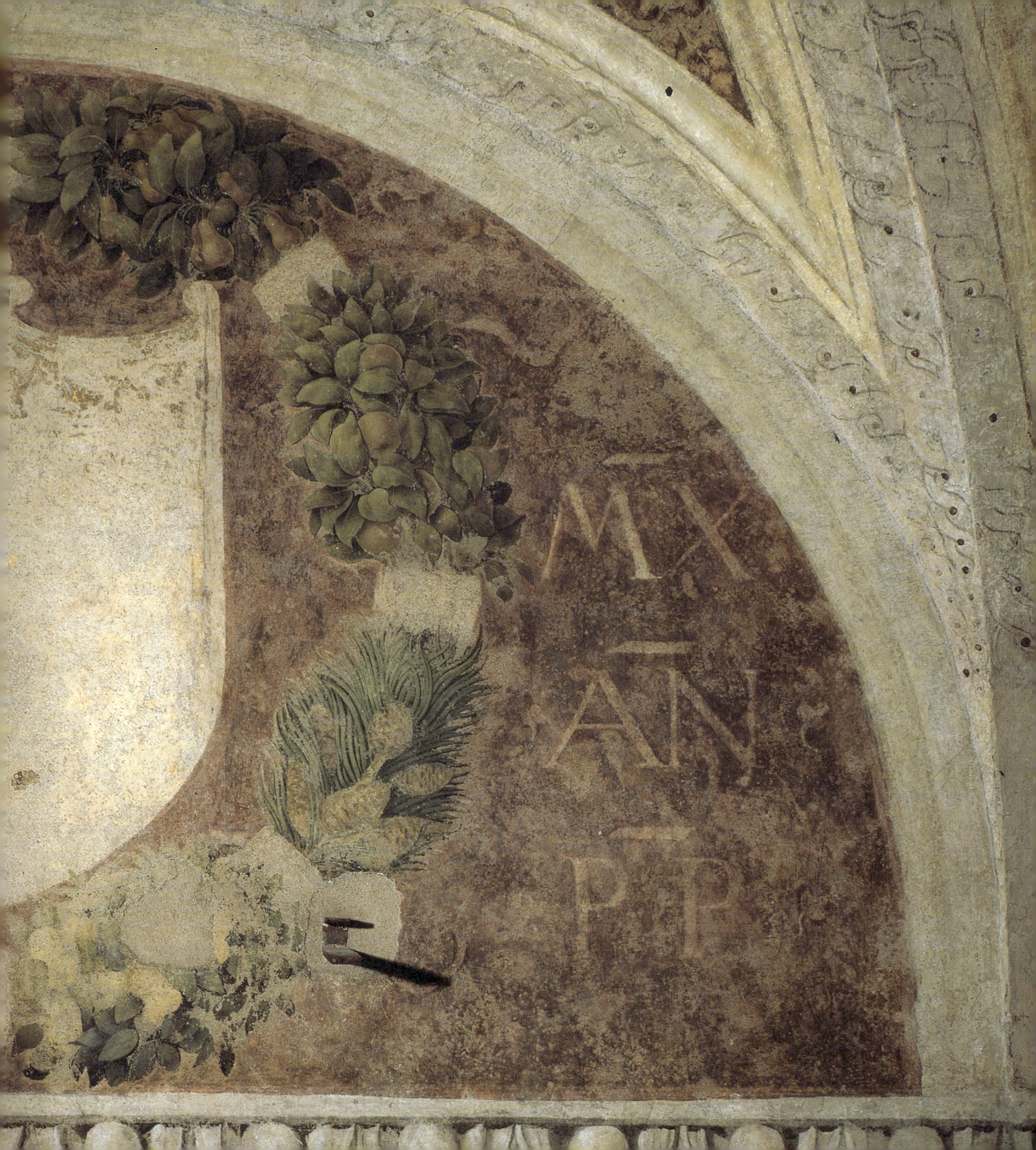
MX
AN
PP

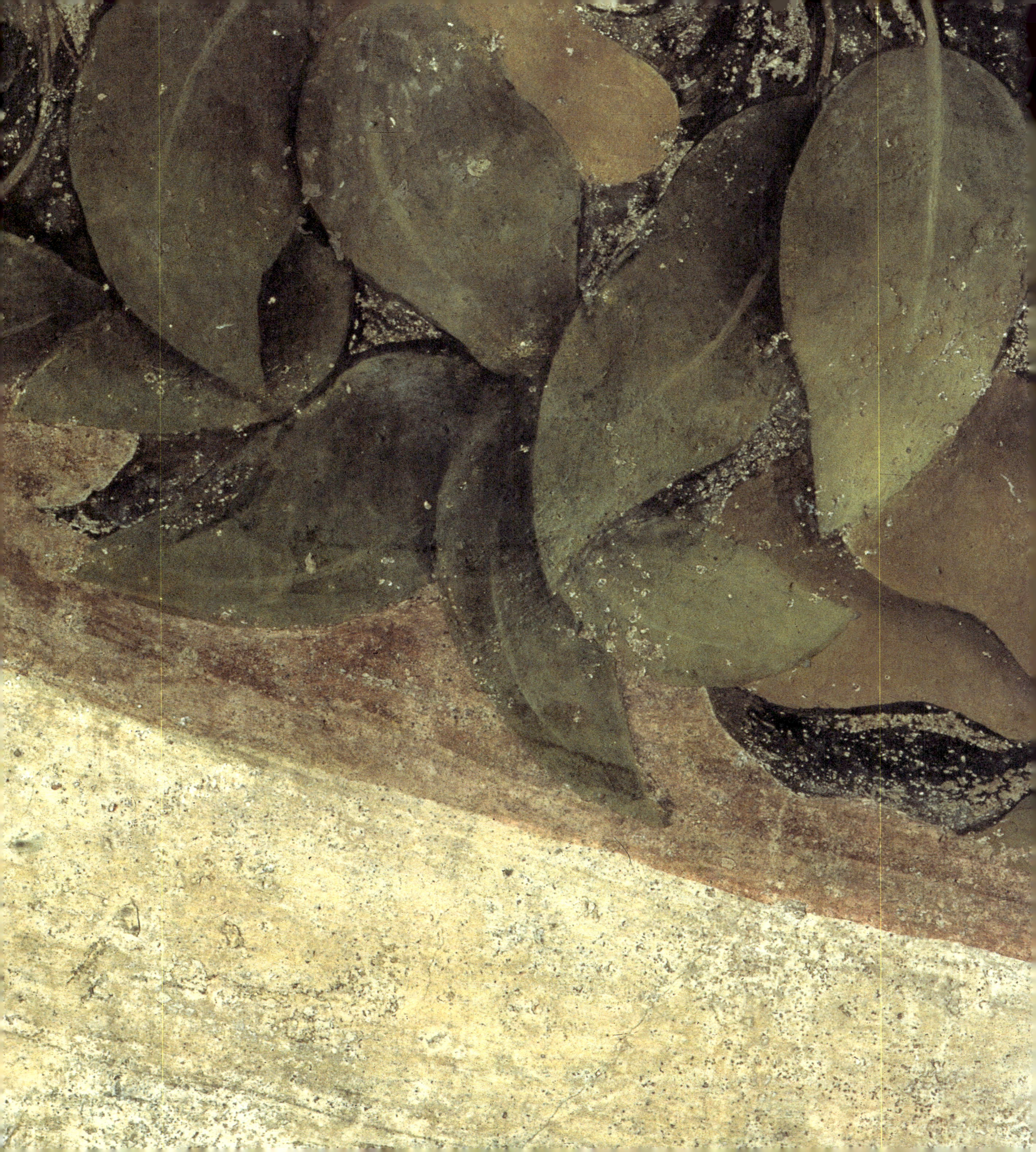

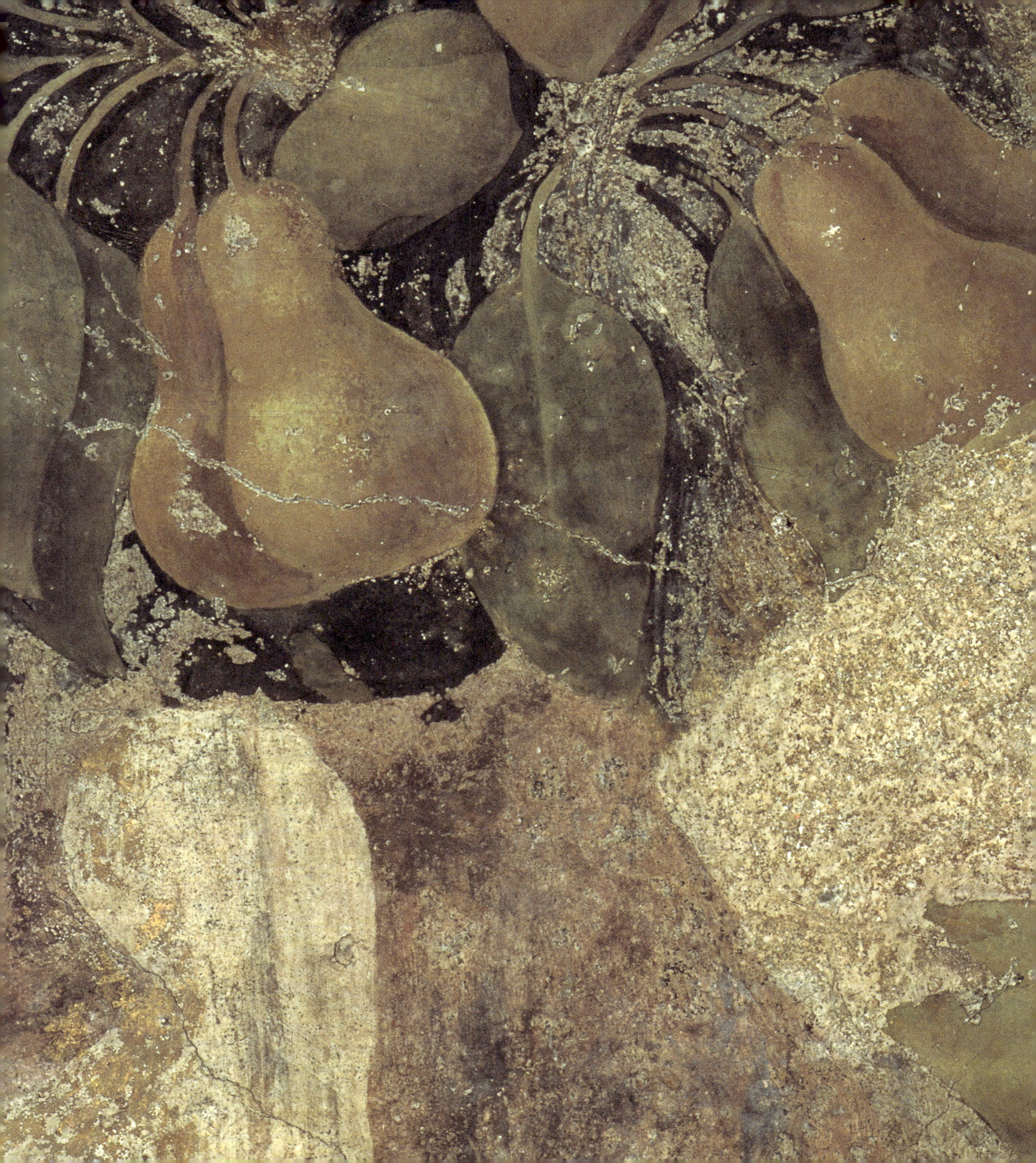

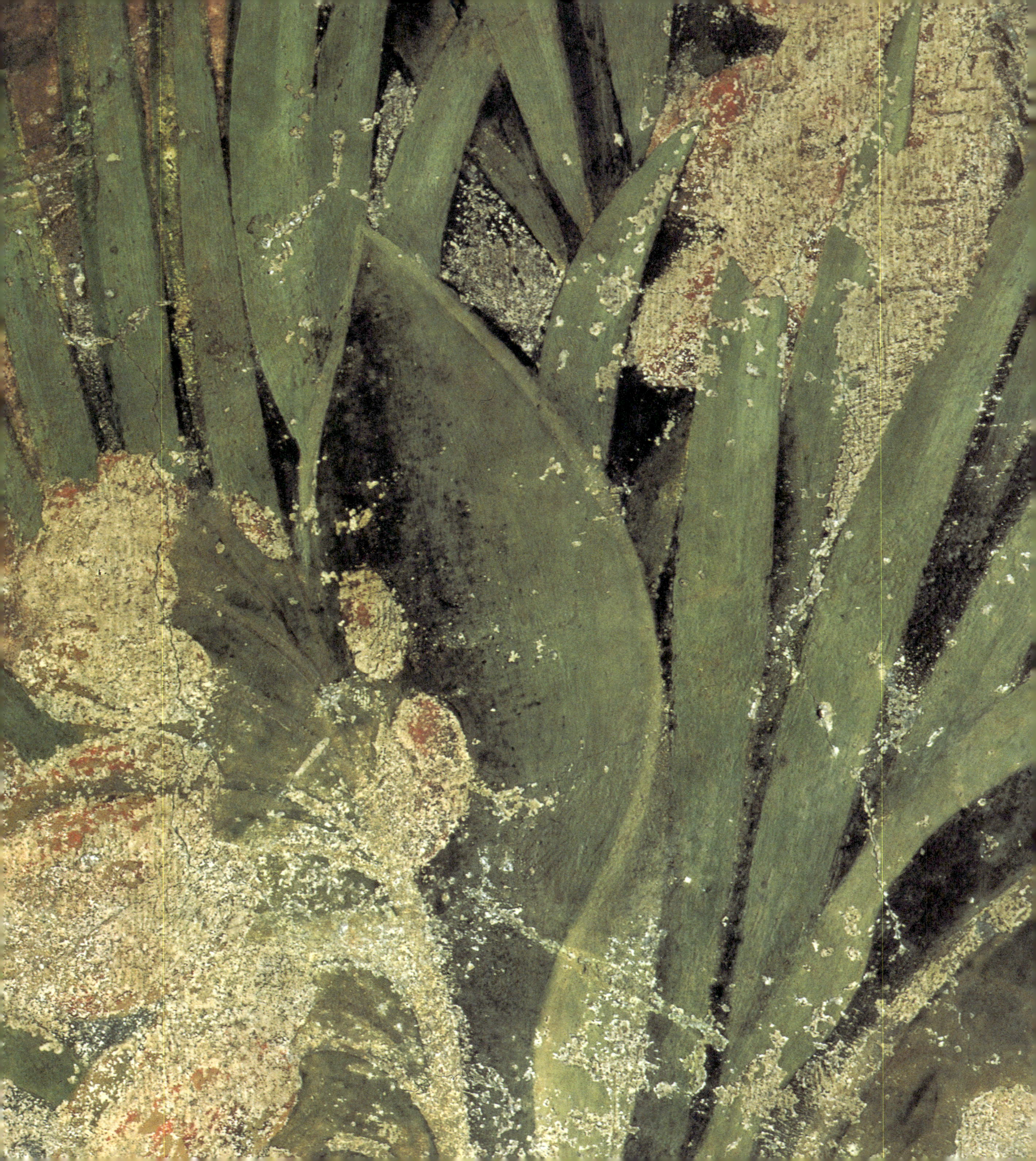

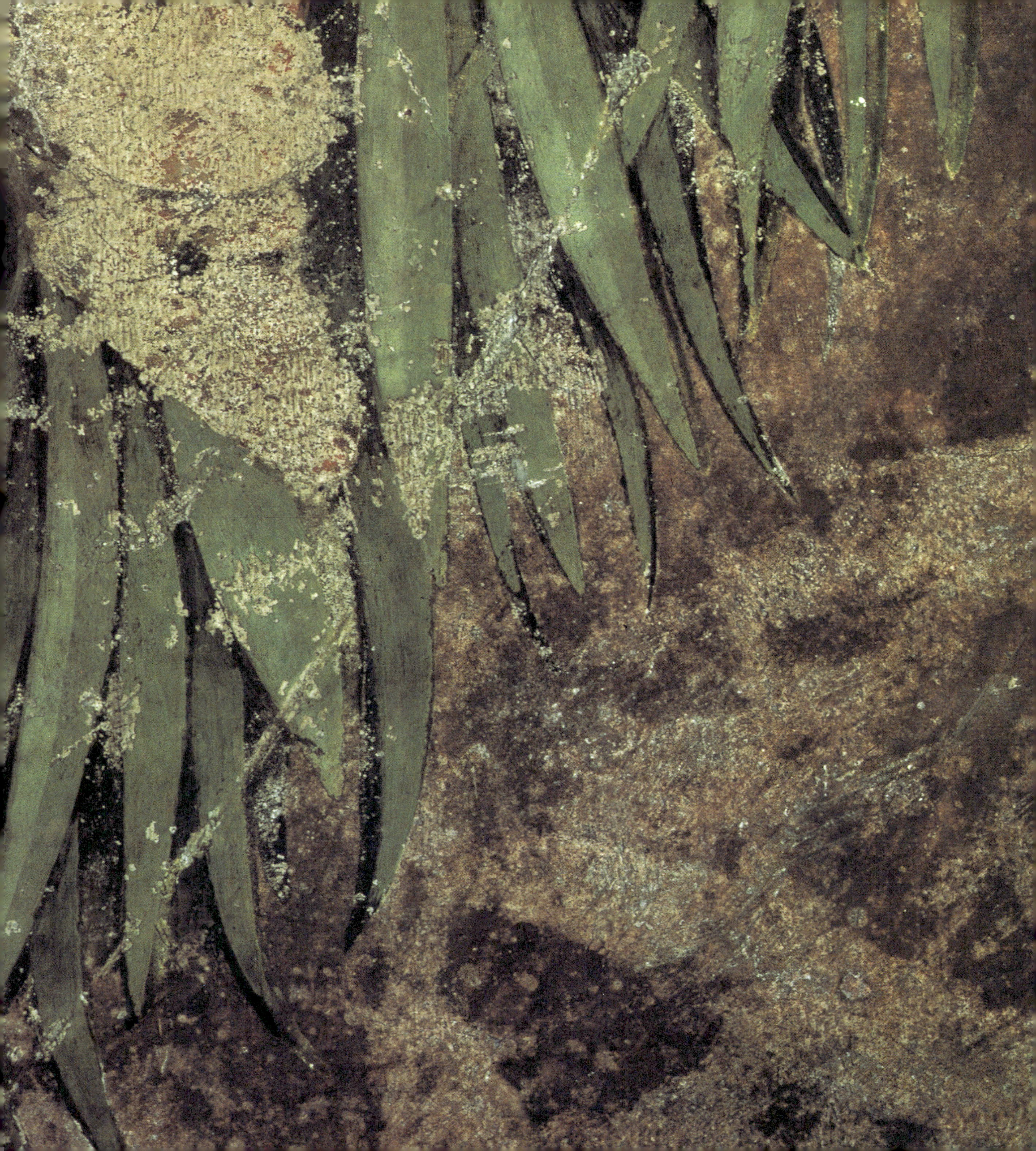

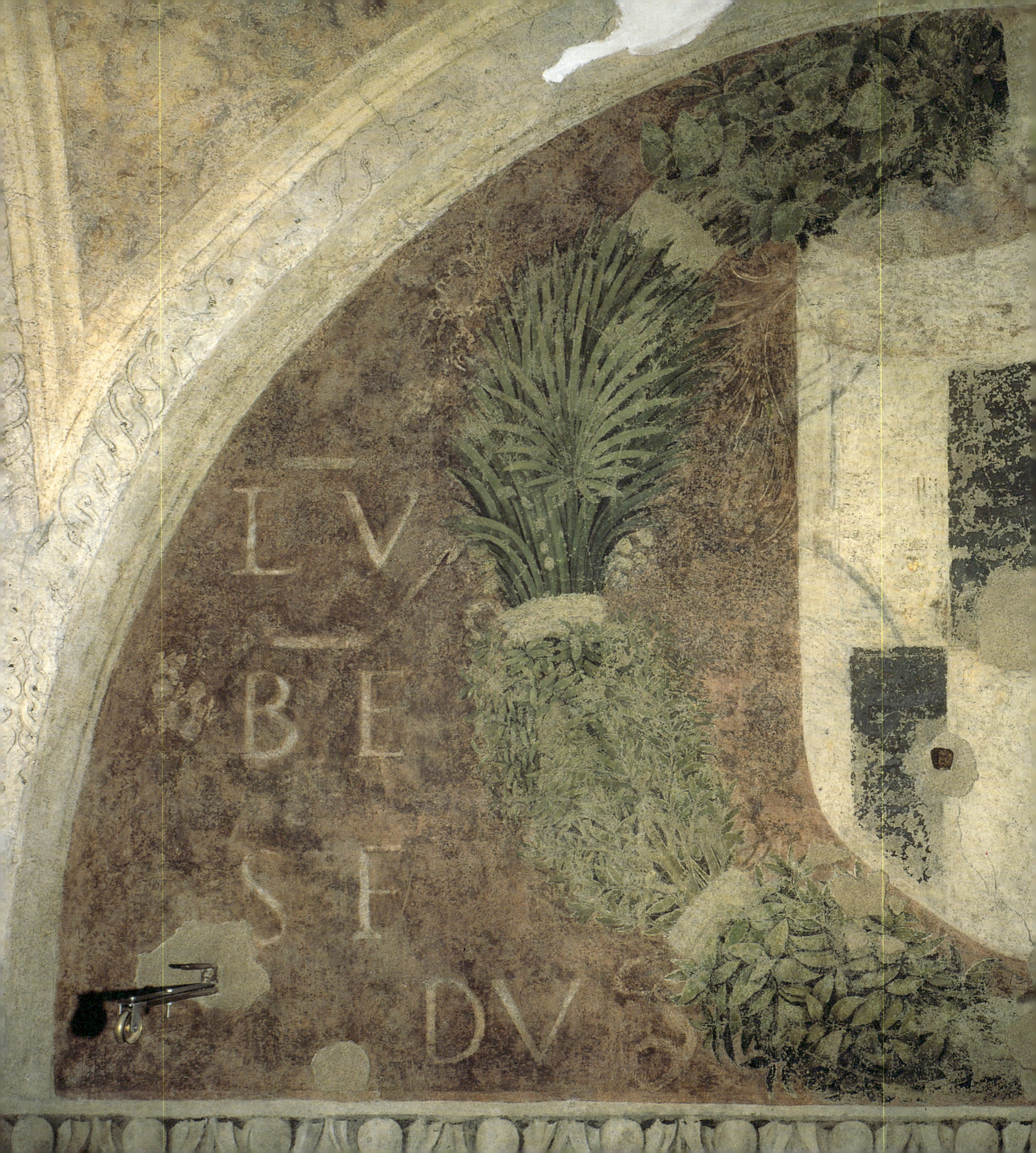
LV
BE
SF
DVS

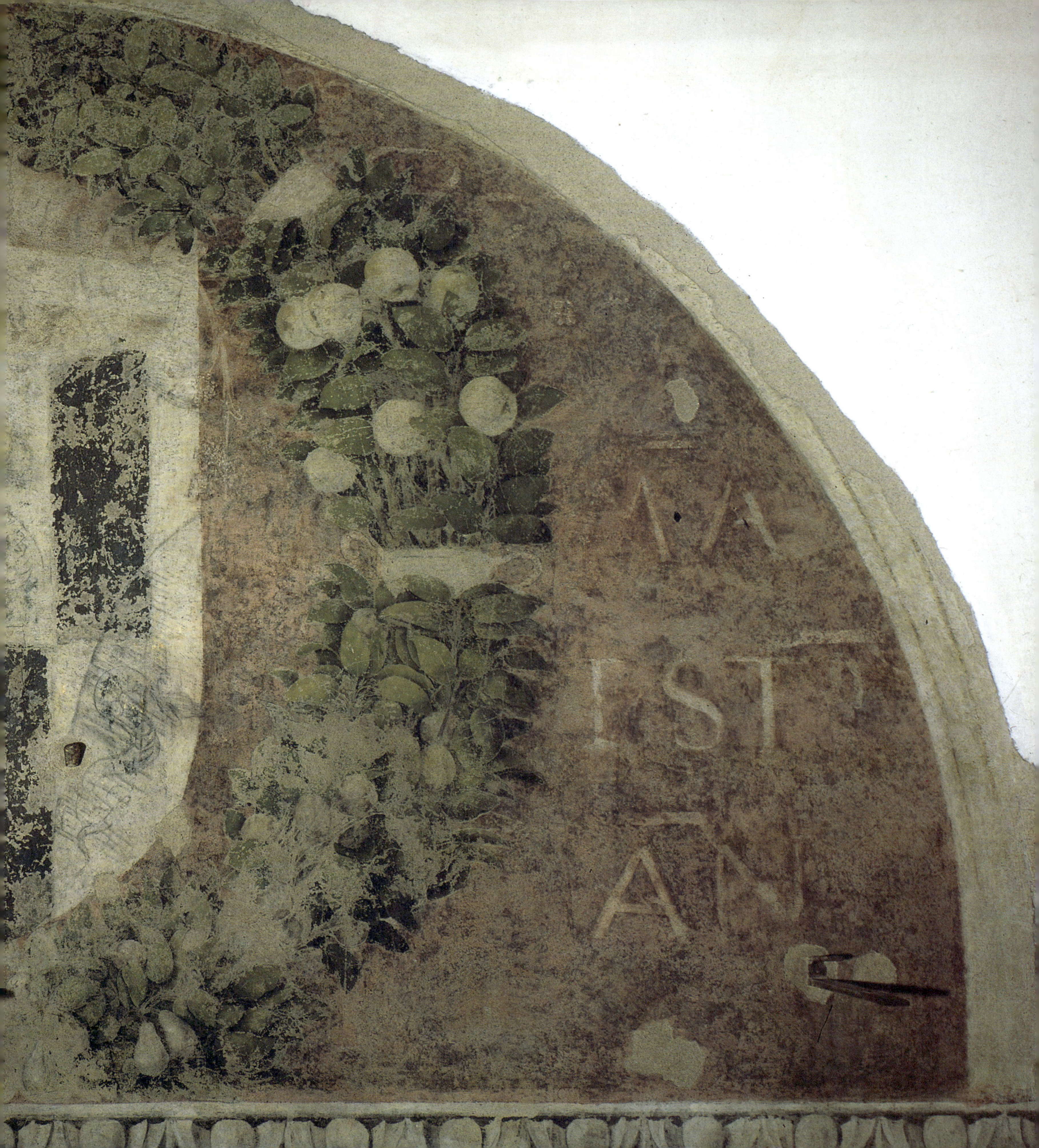

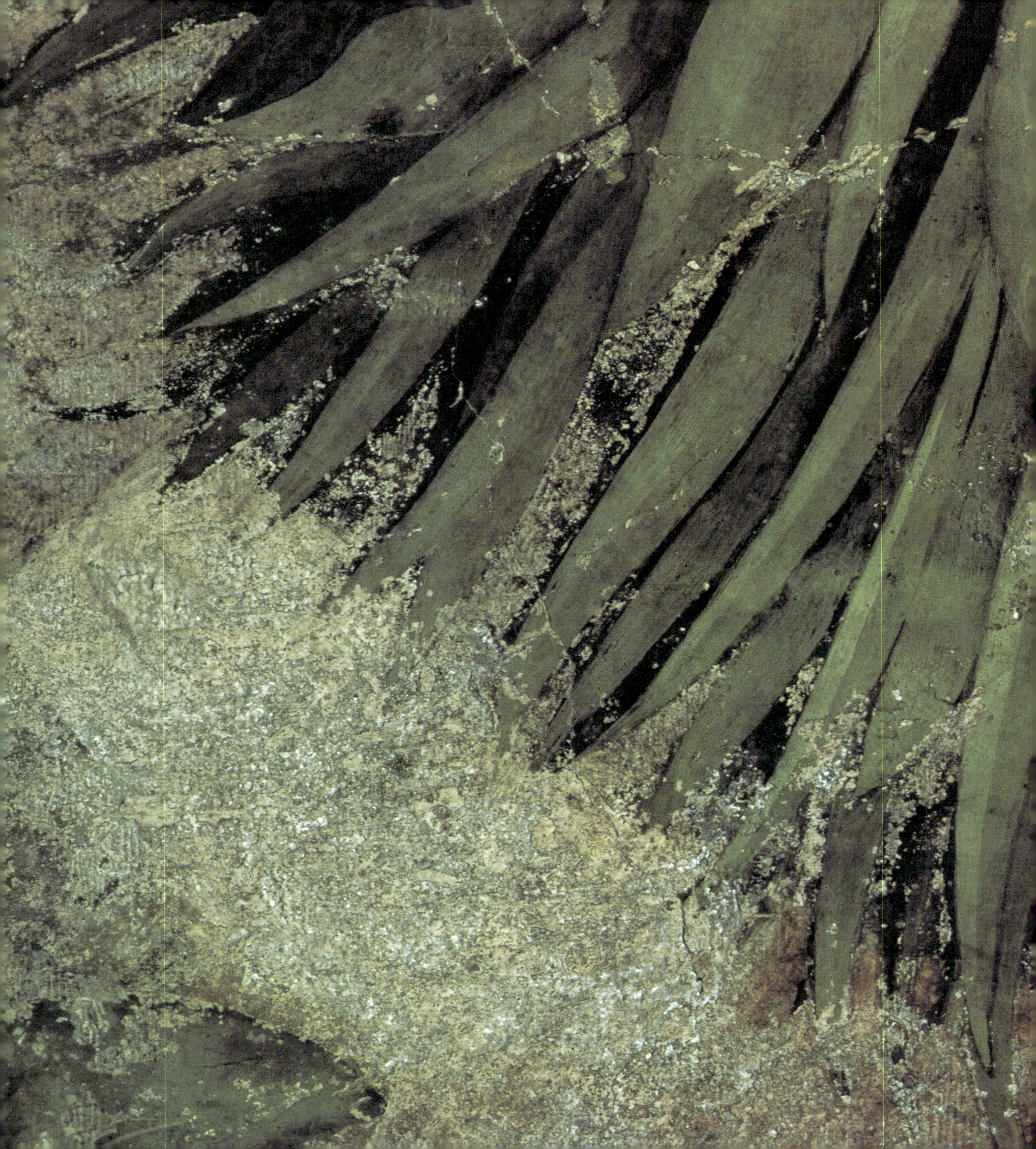

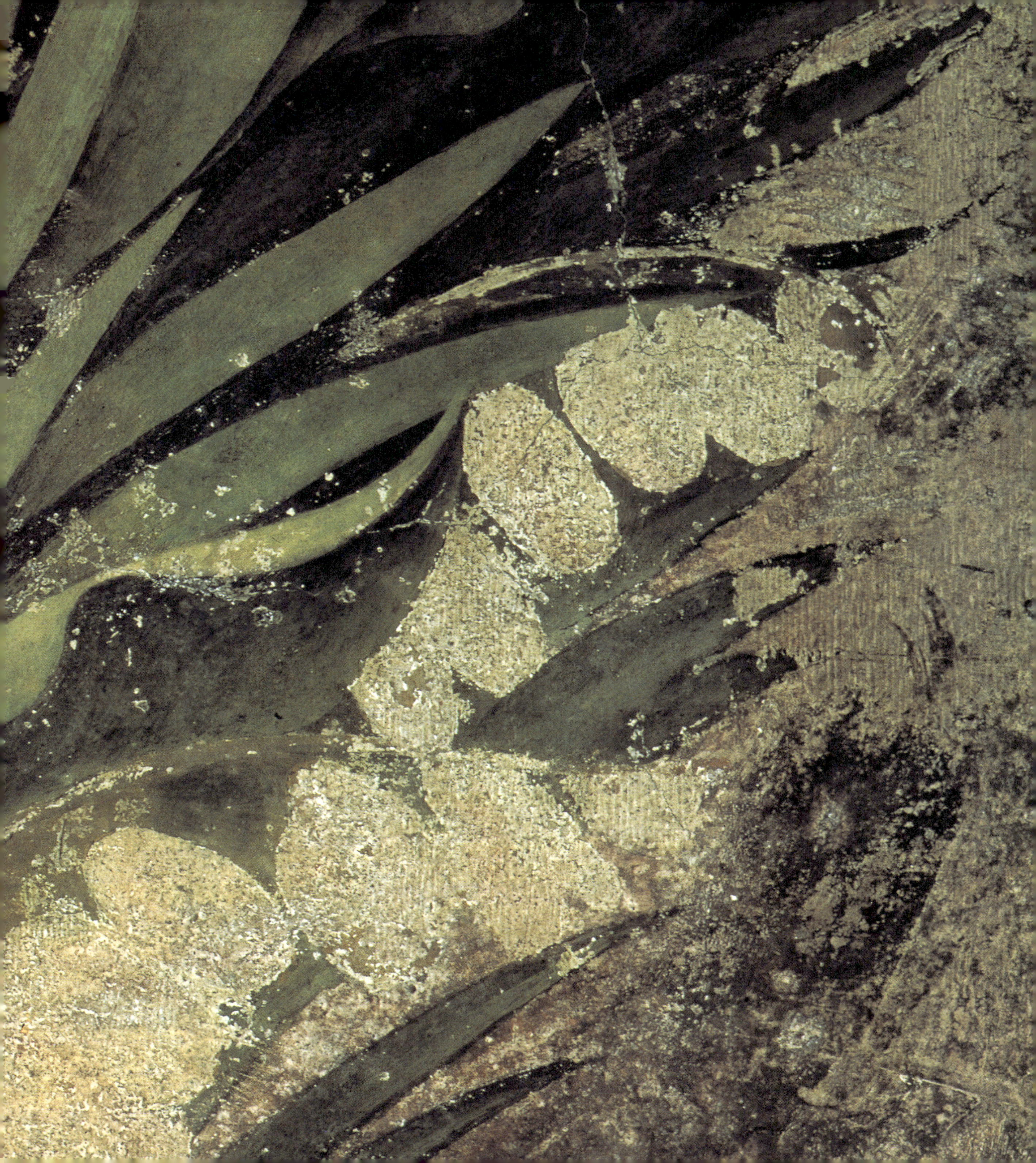

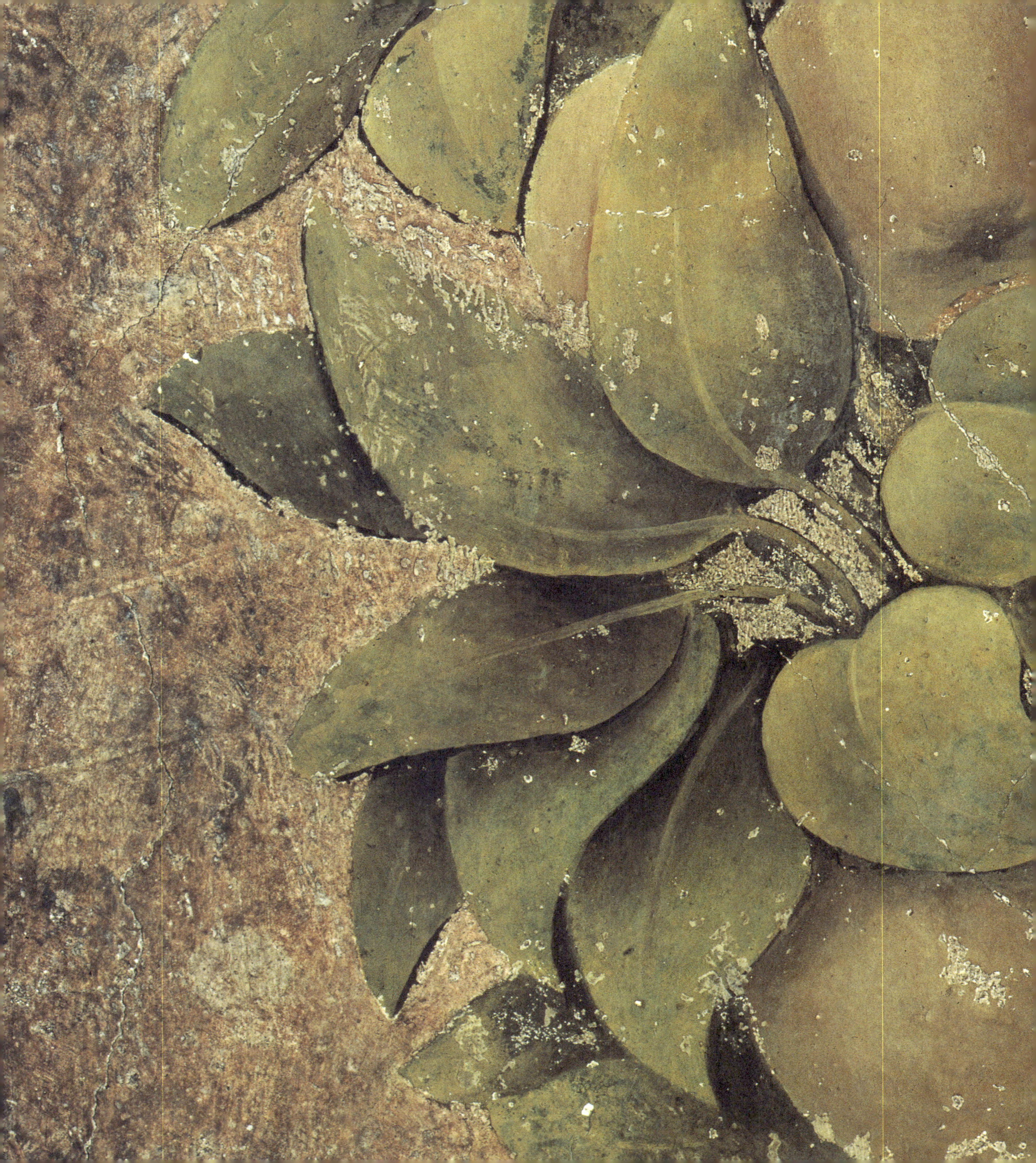

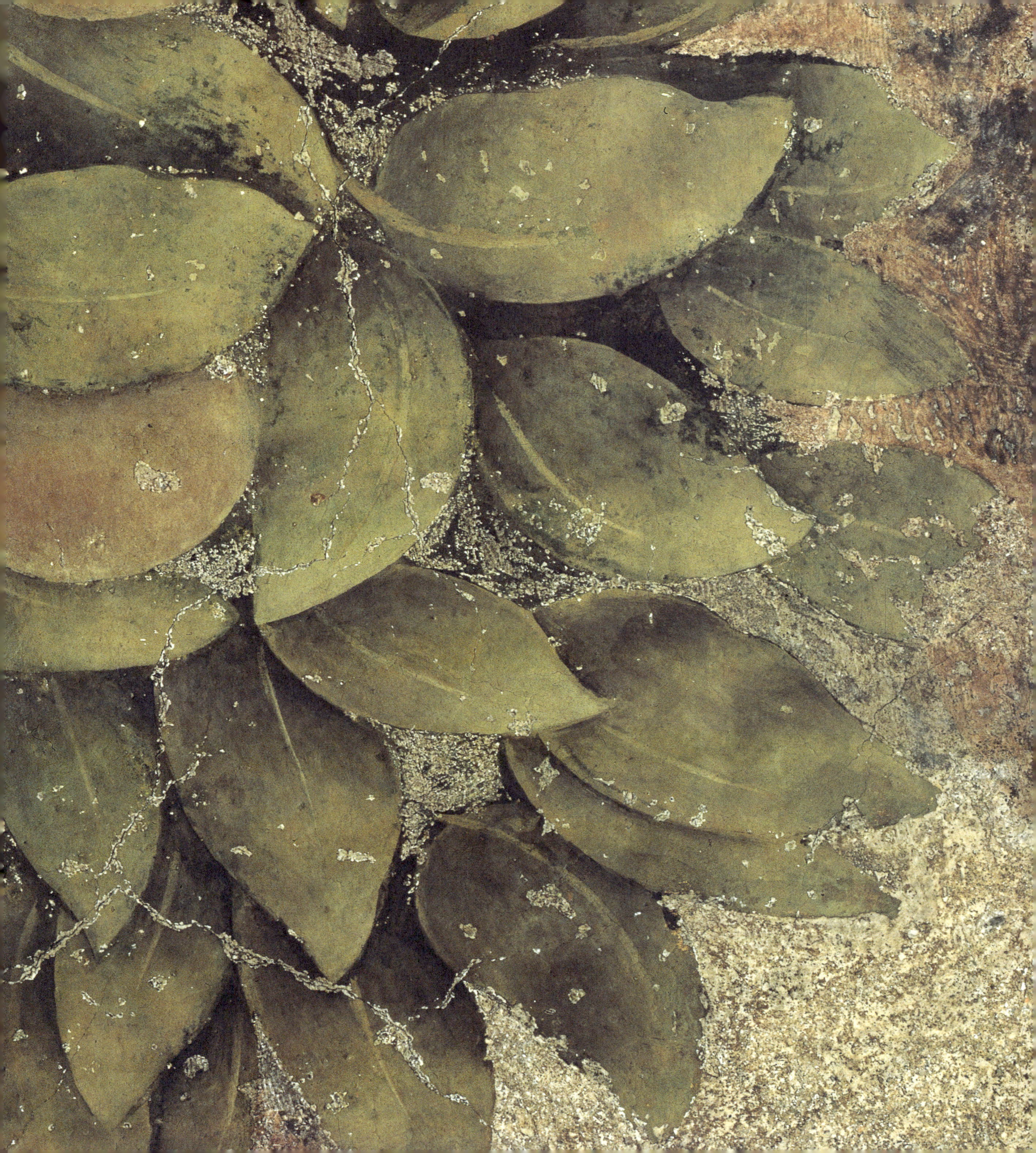

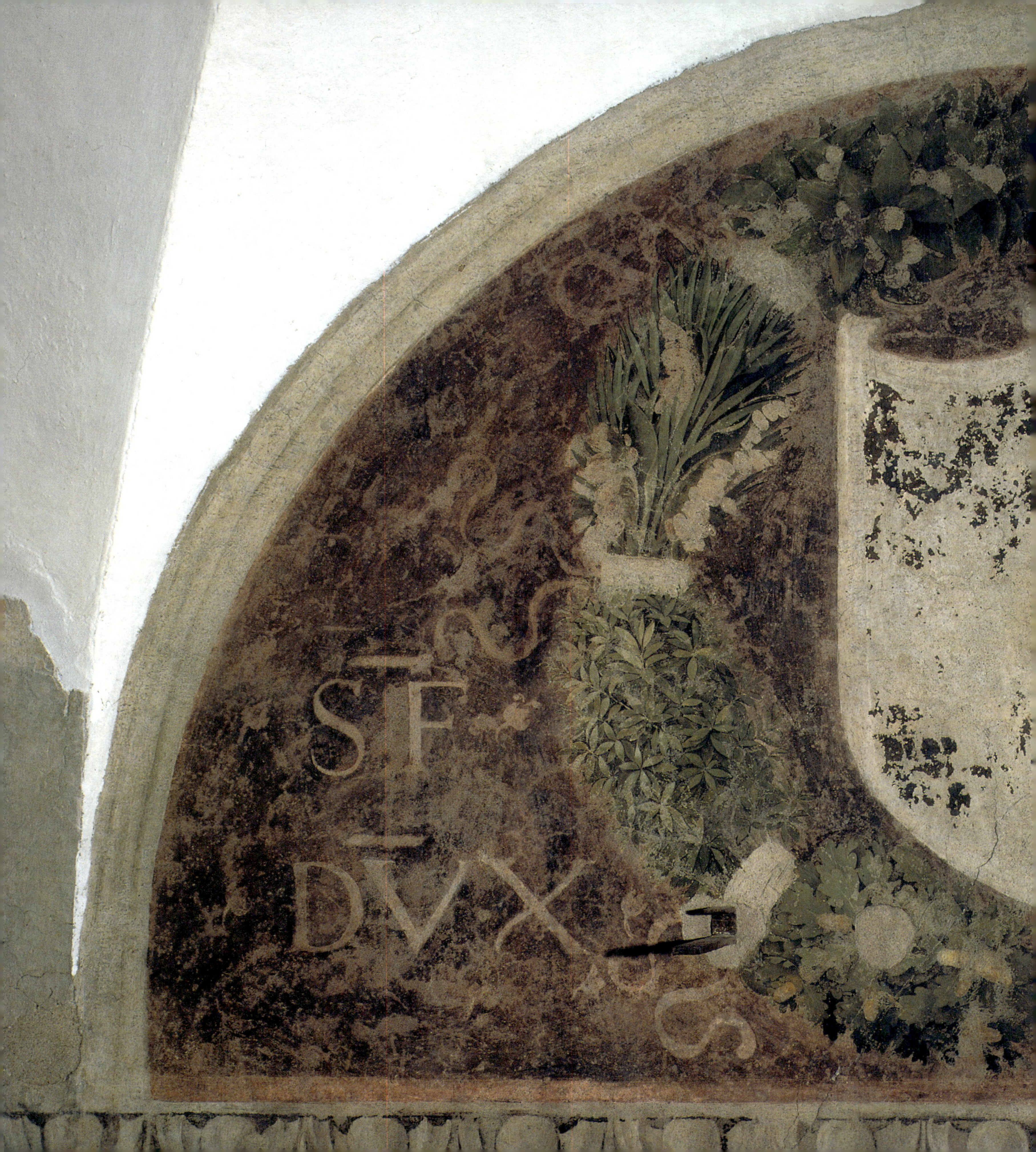
SF
DVX

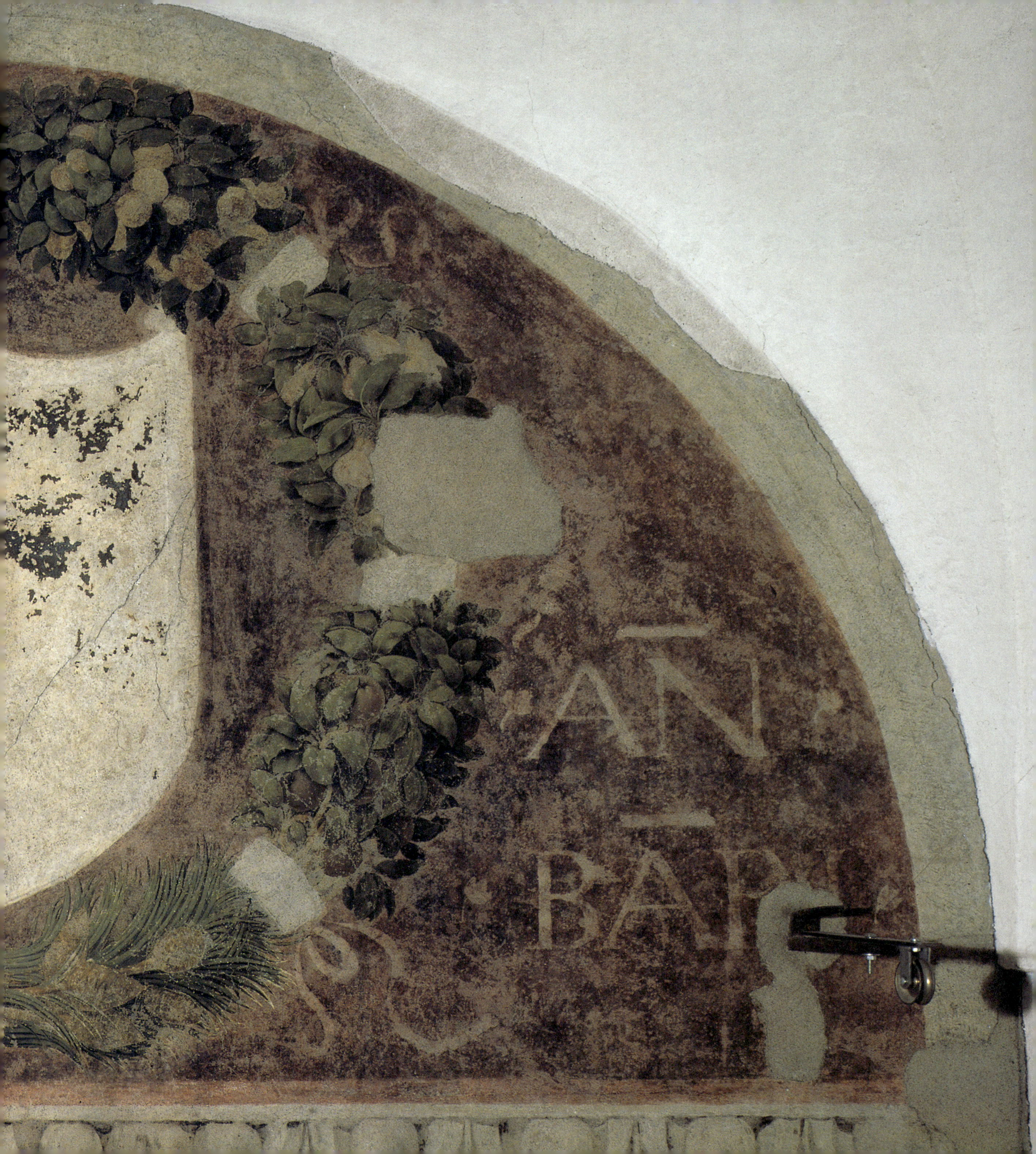
ĀN
BAP

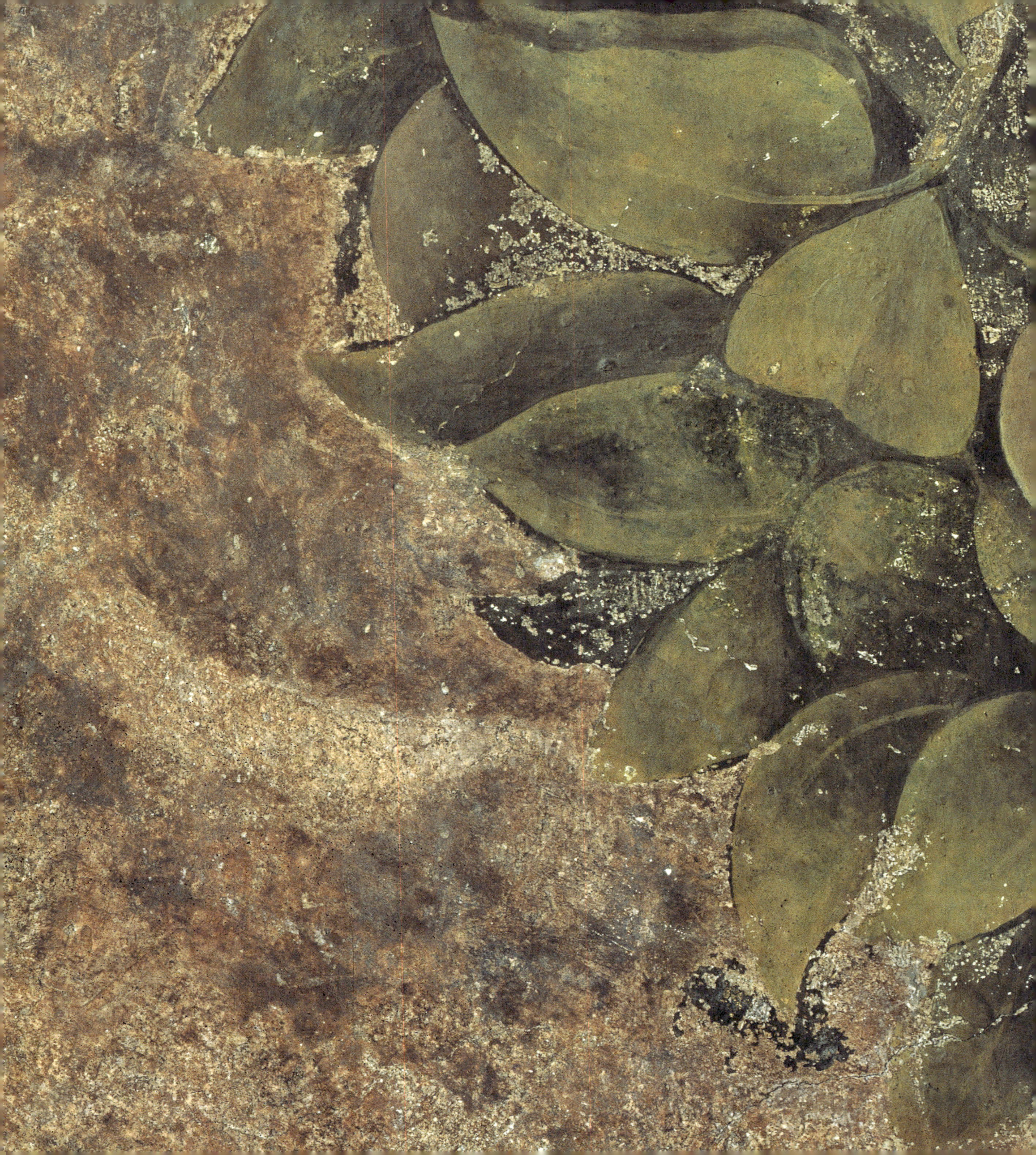

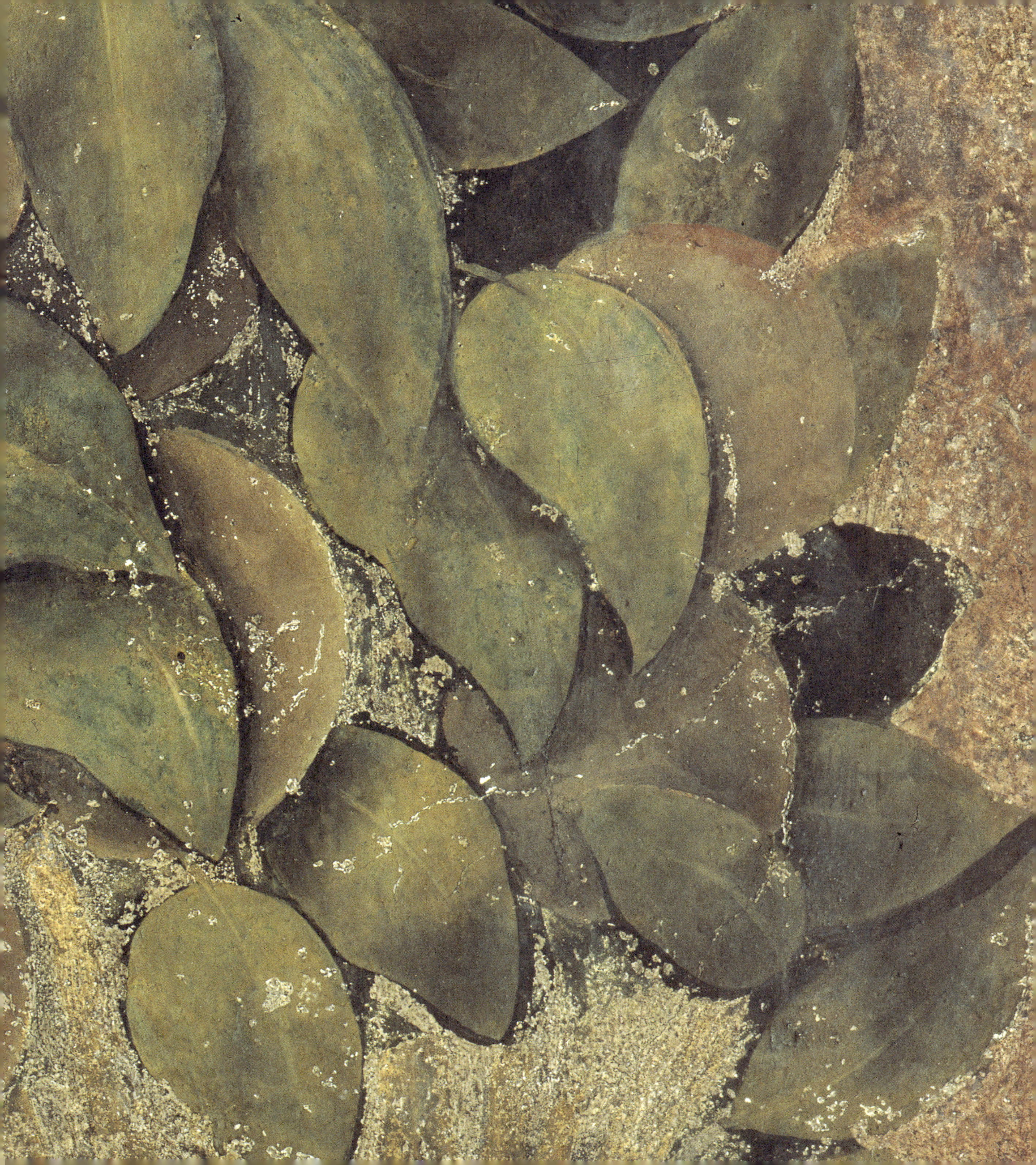

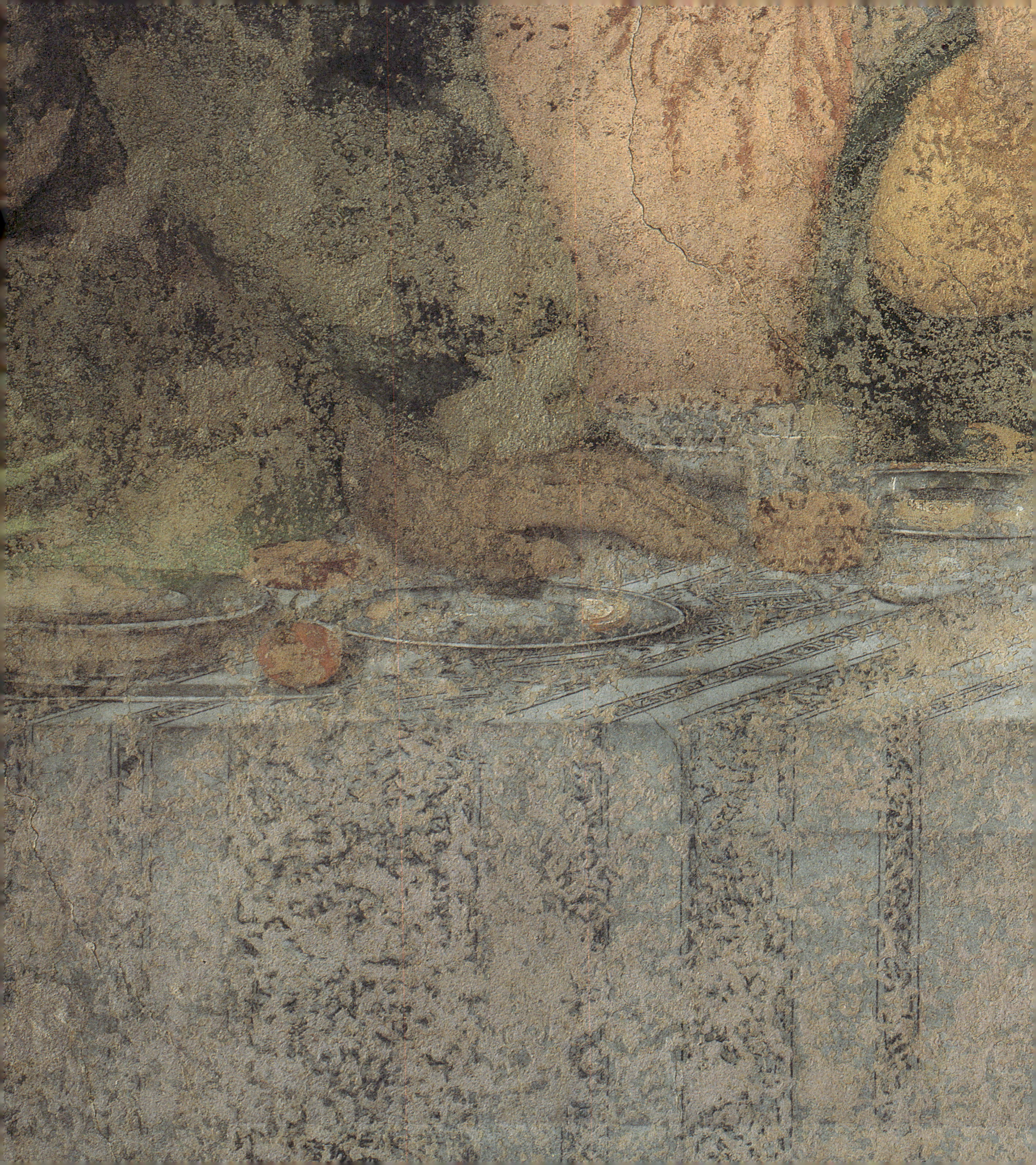

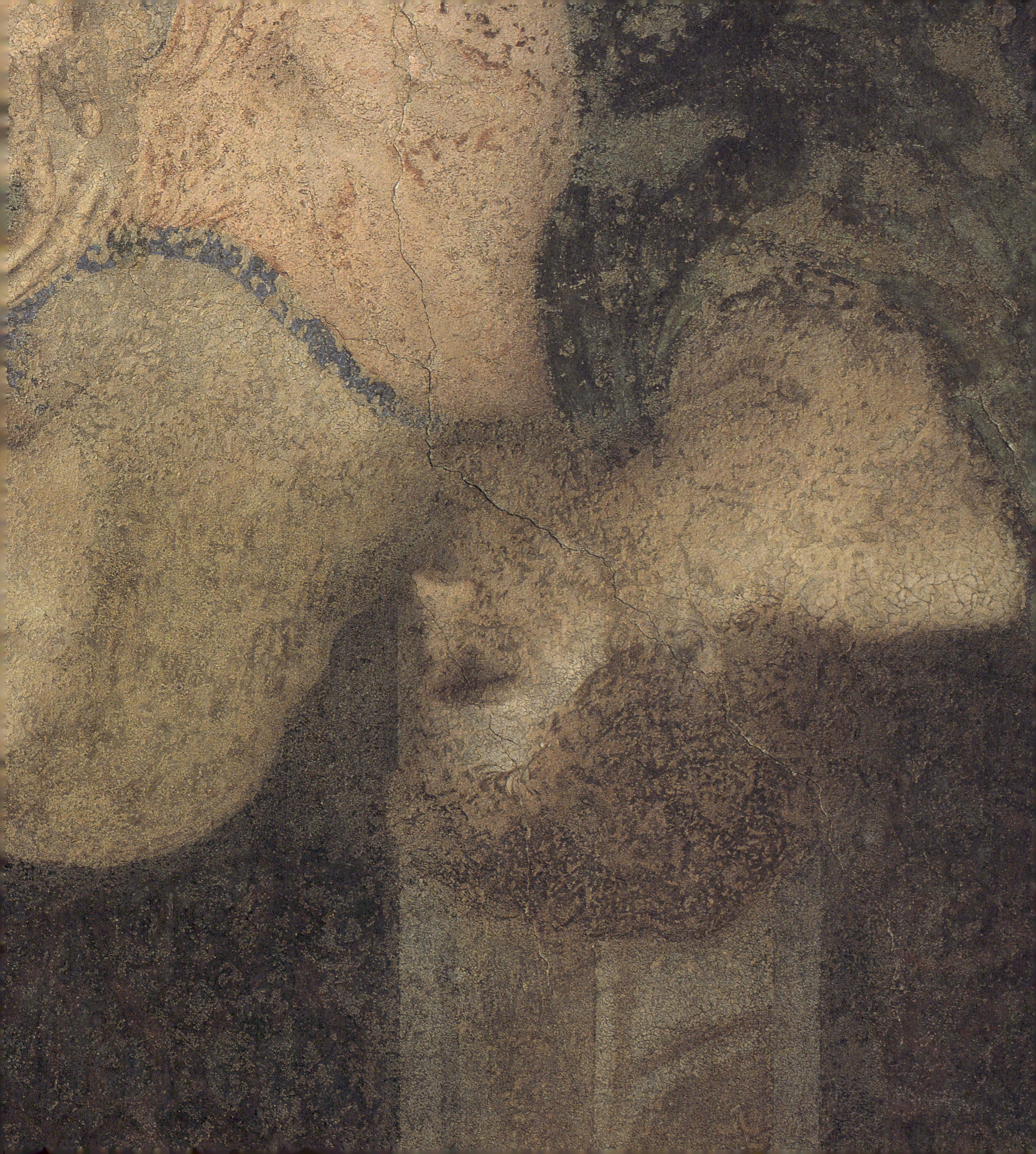

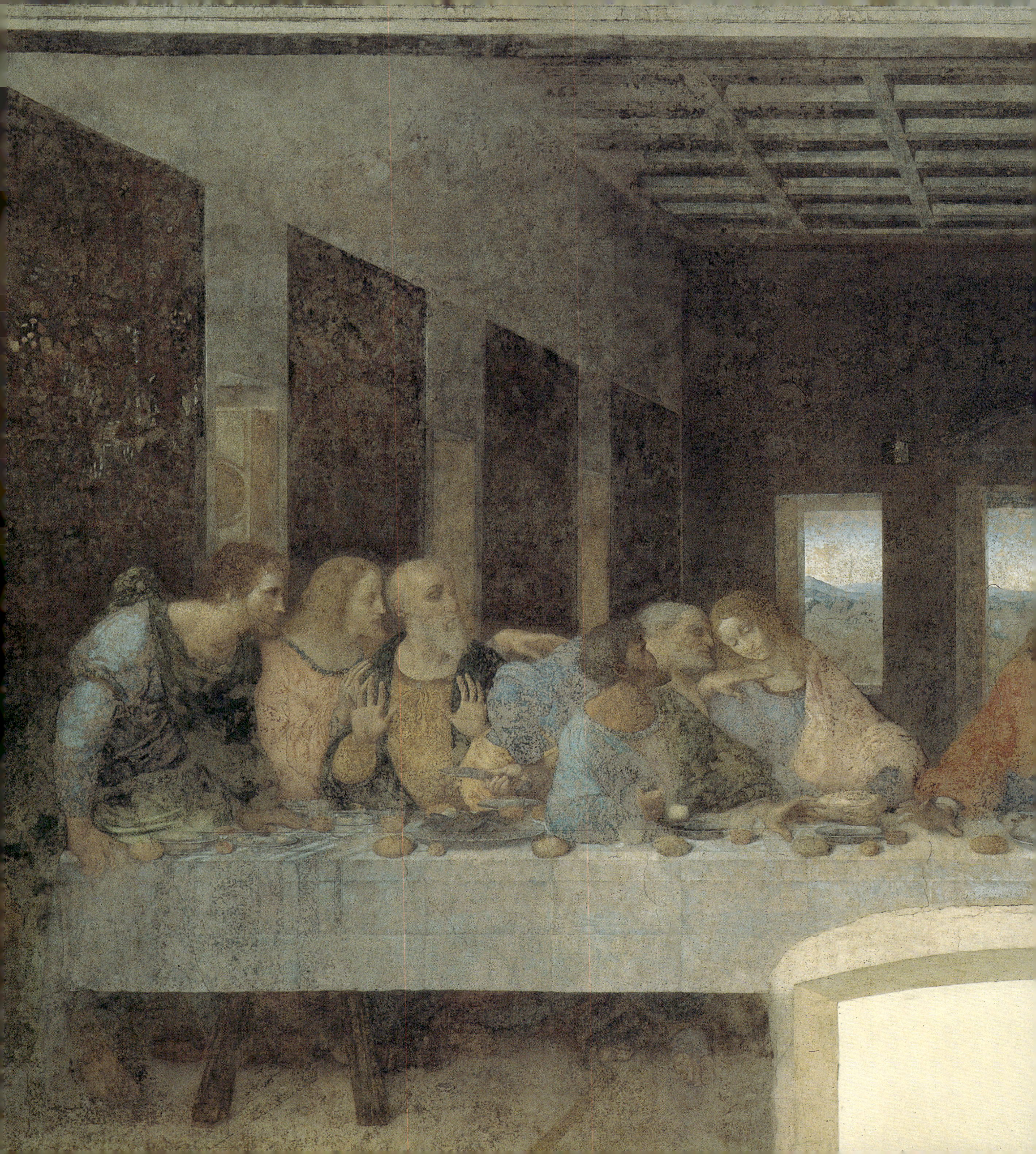

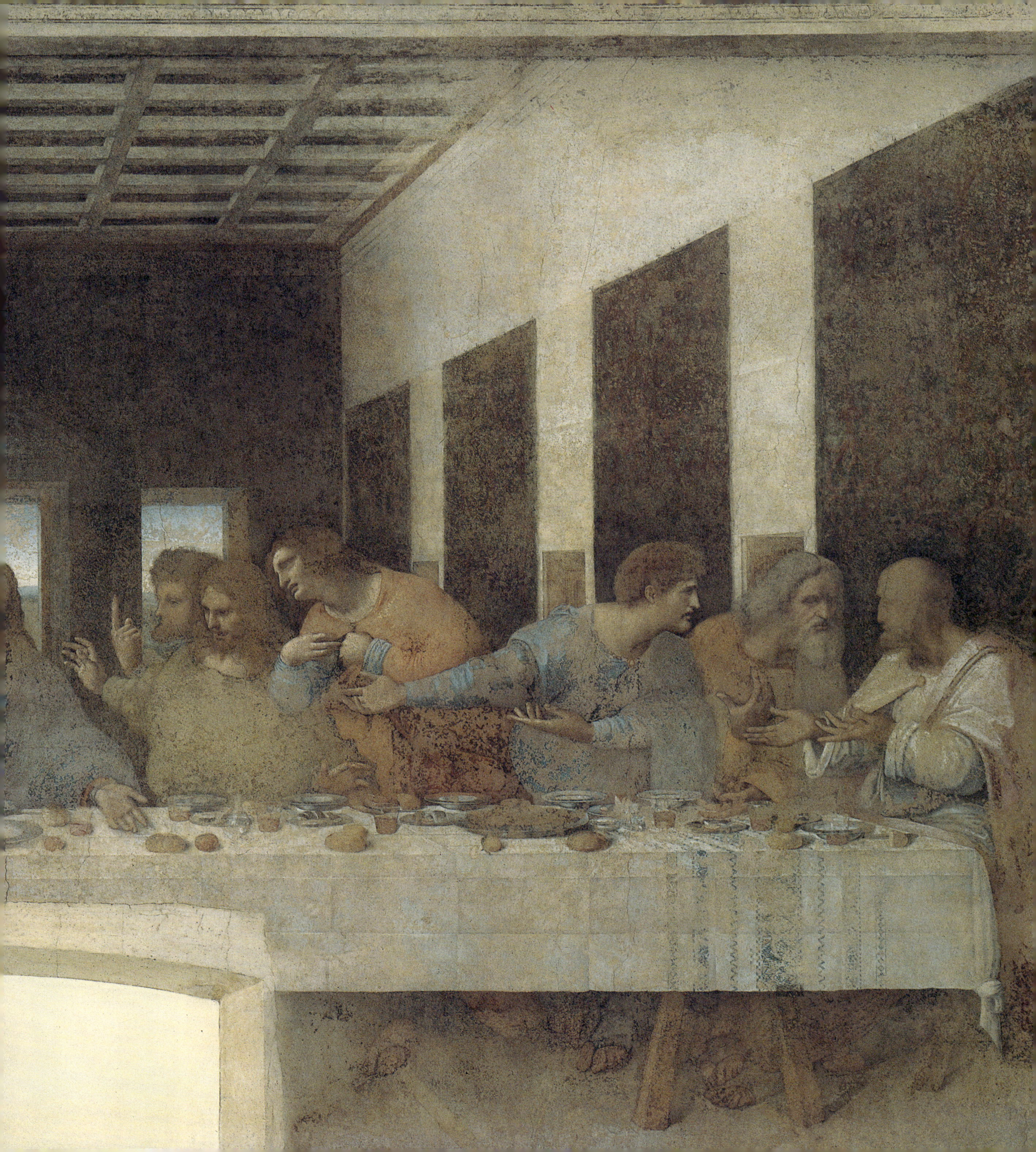

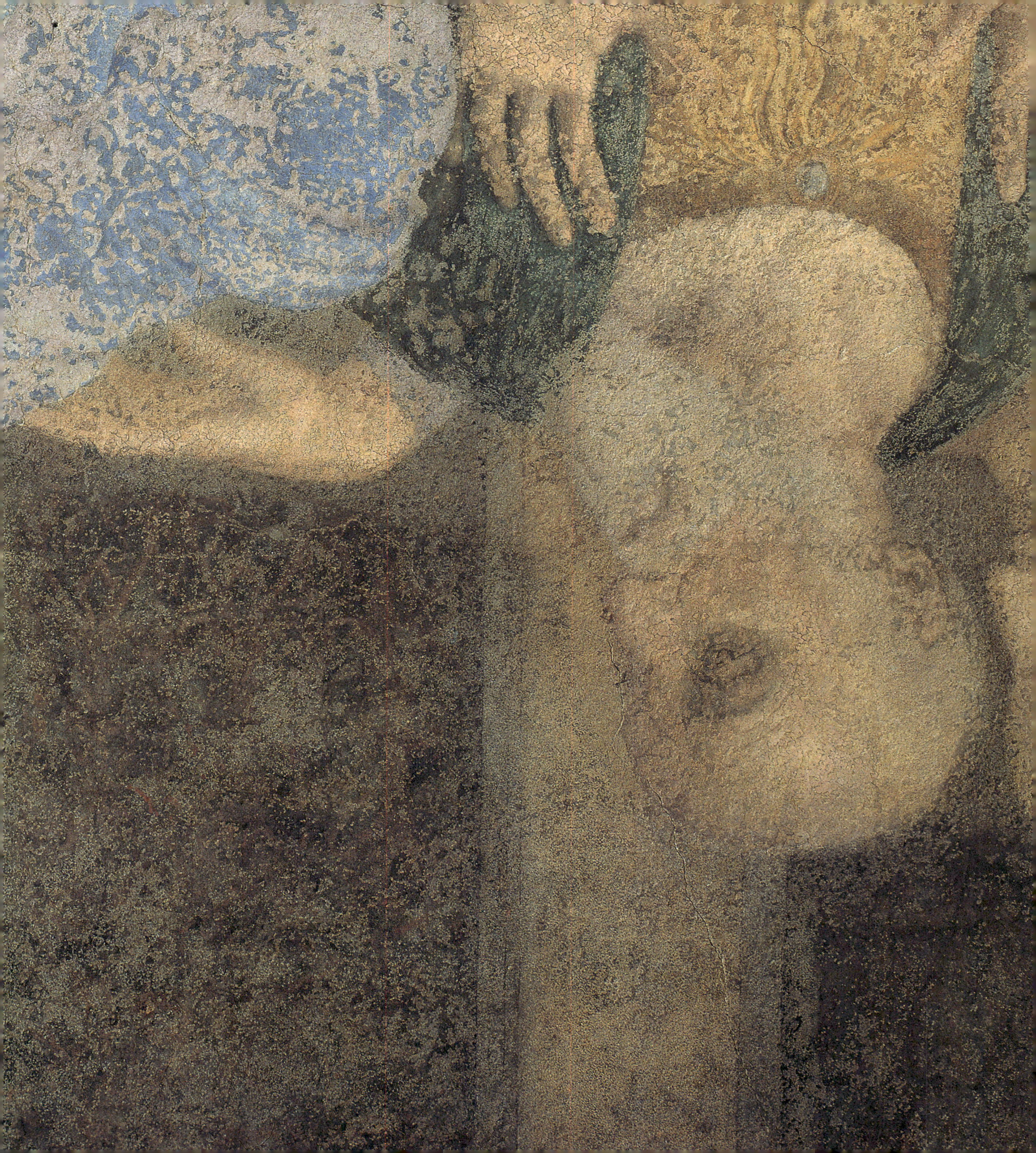

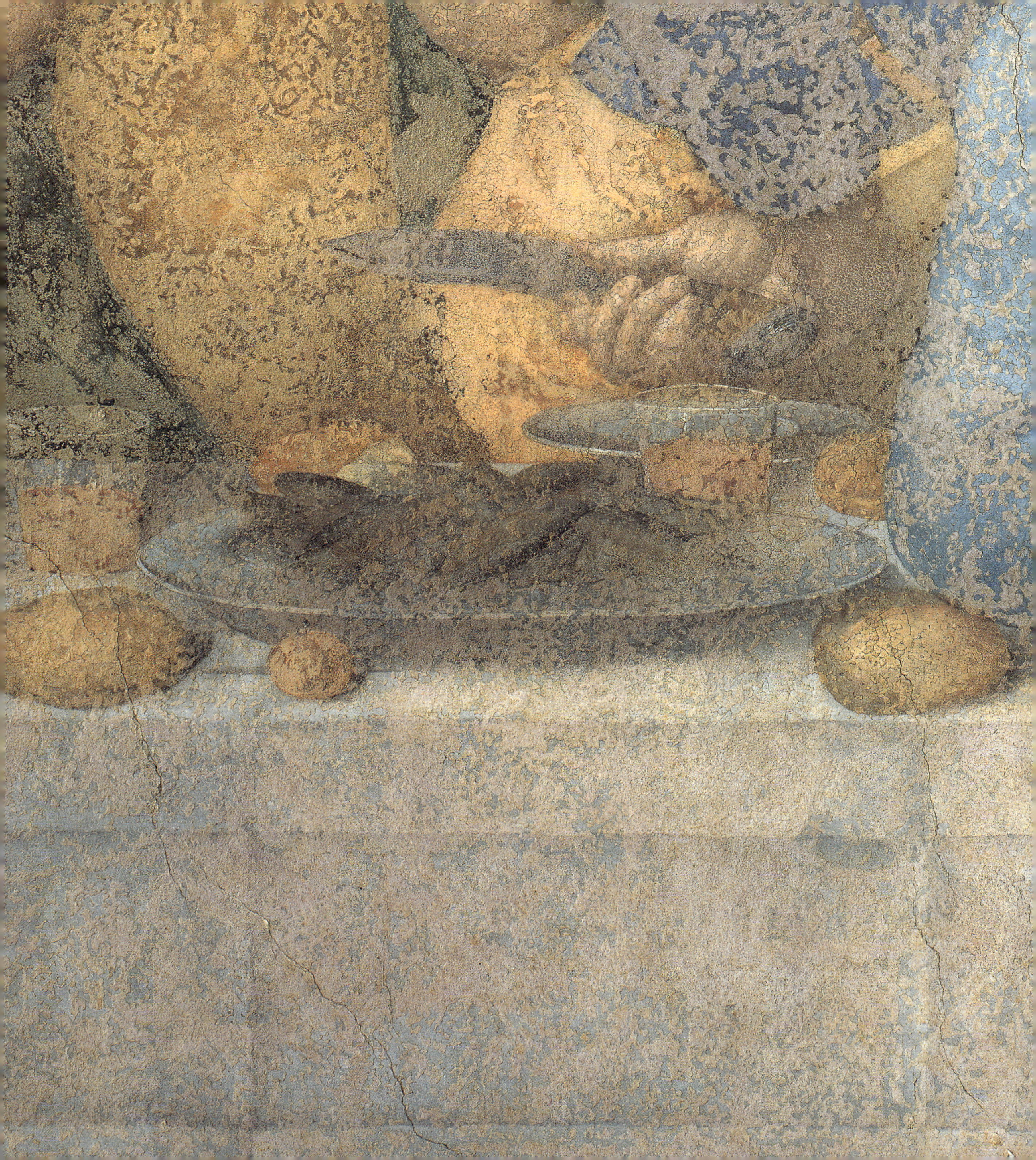

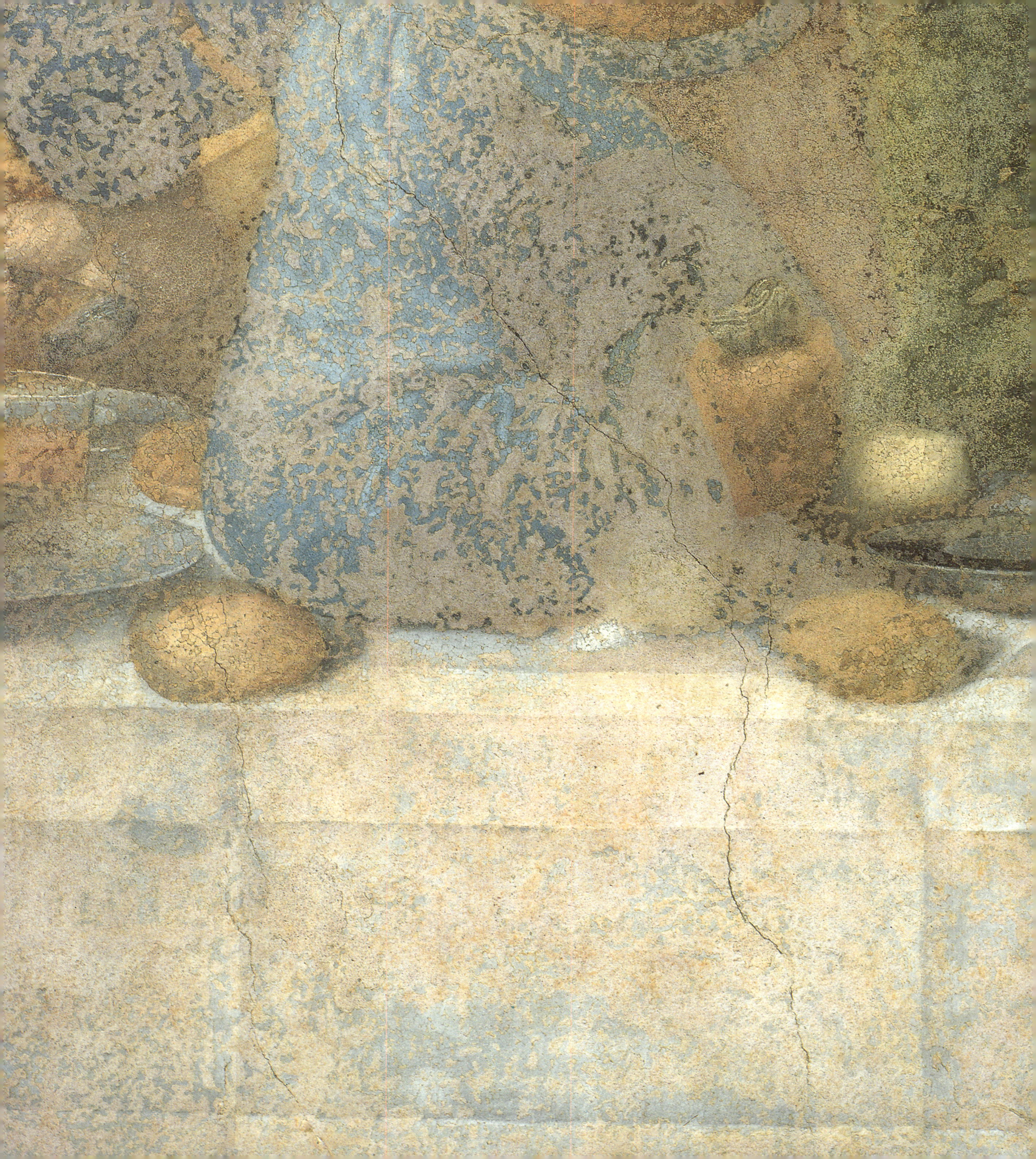

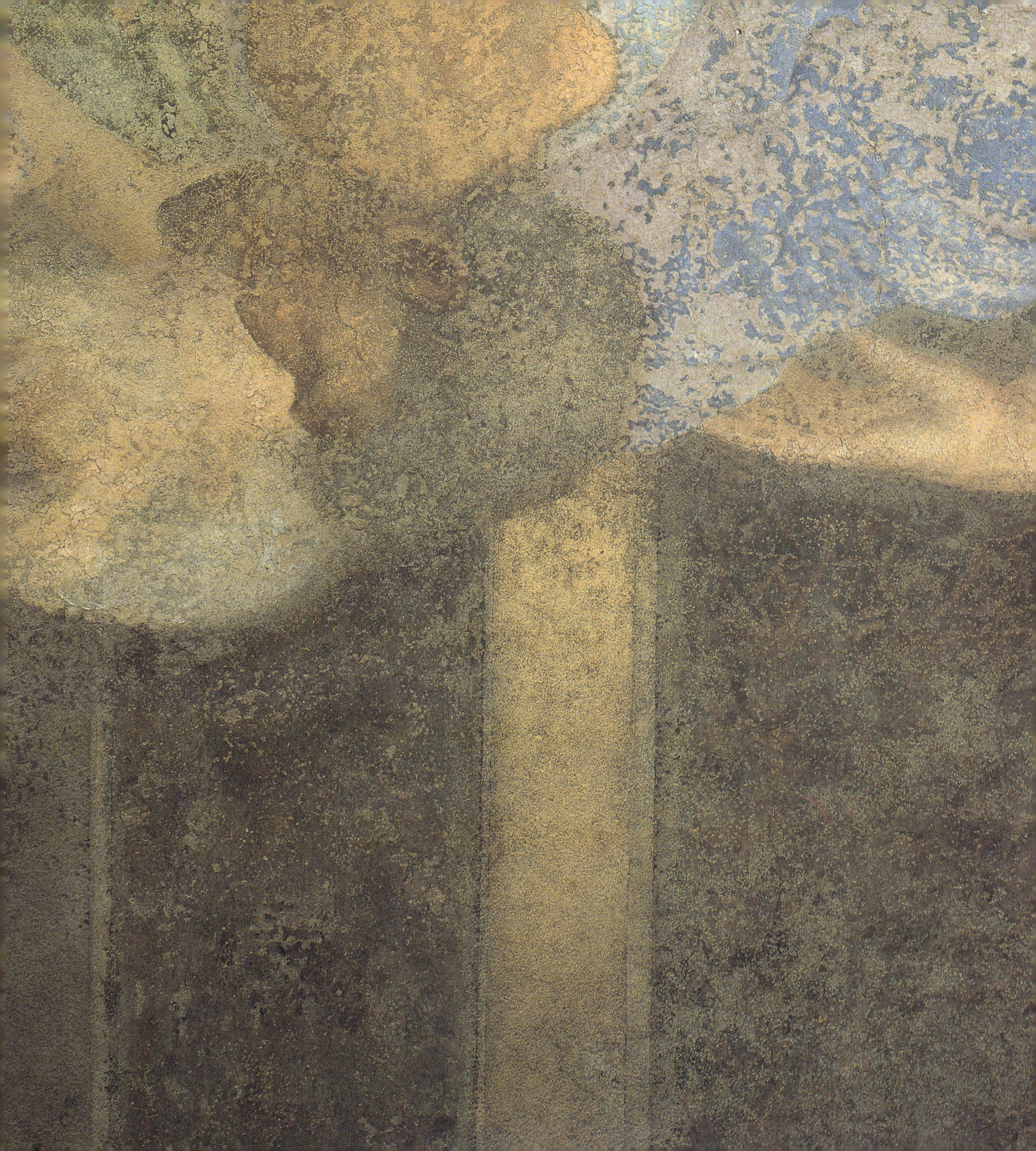

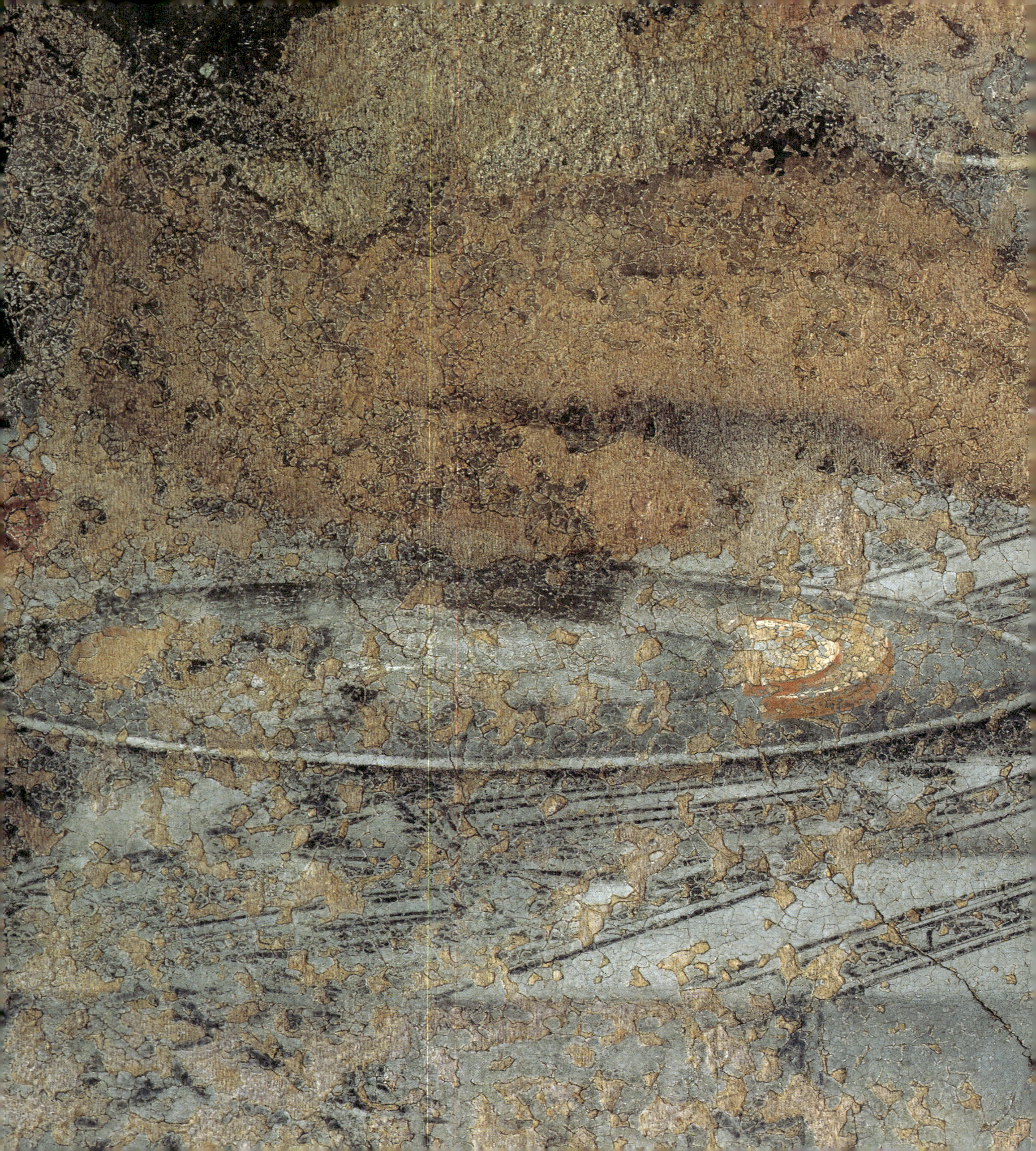

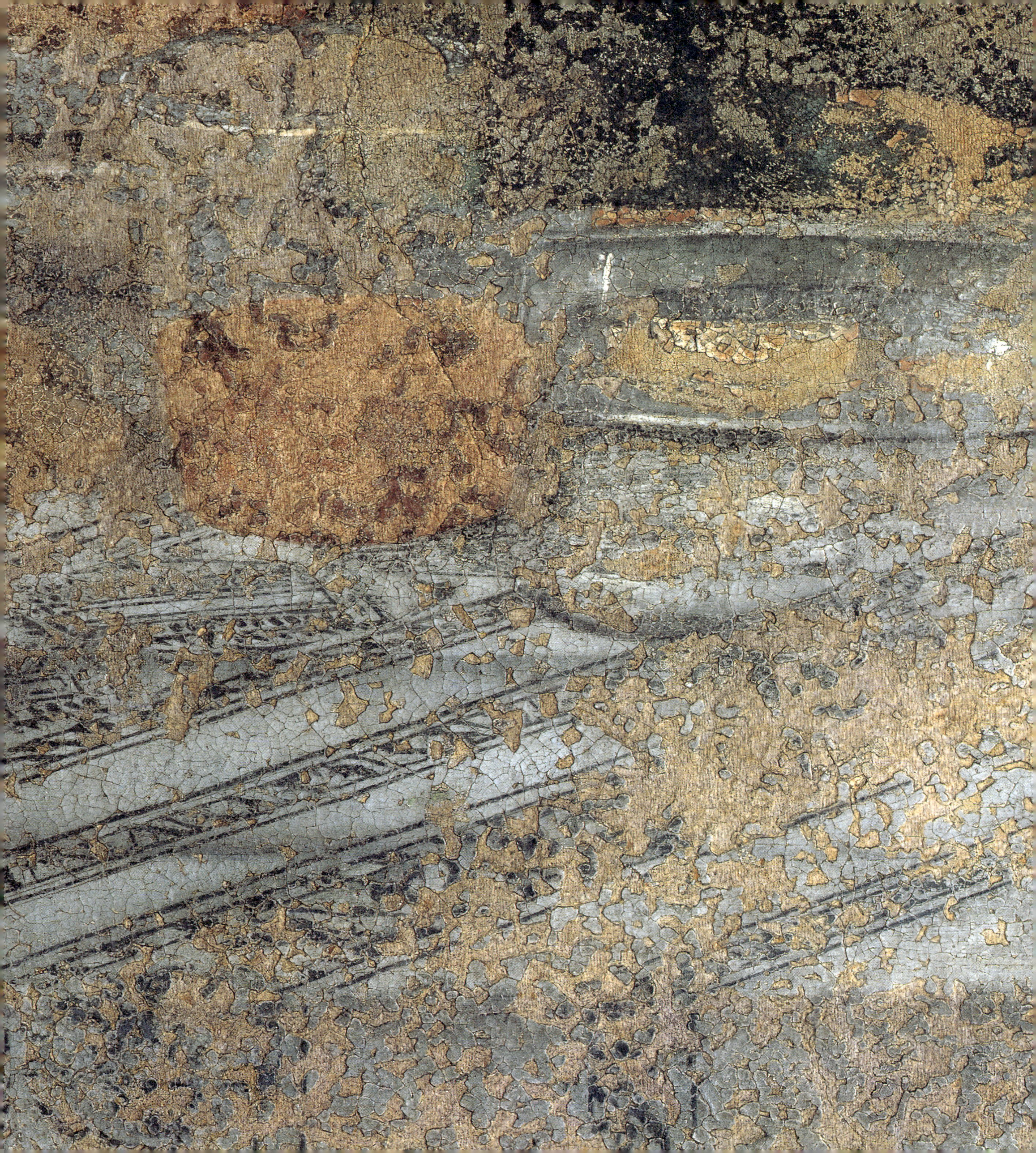

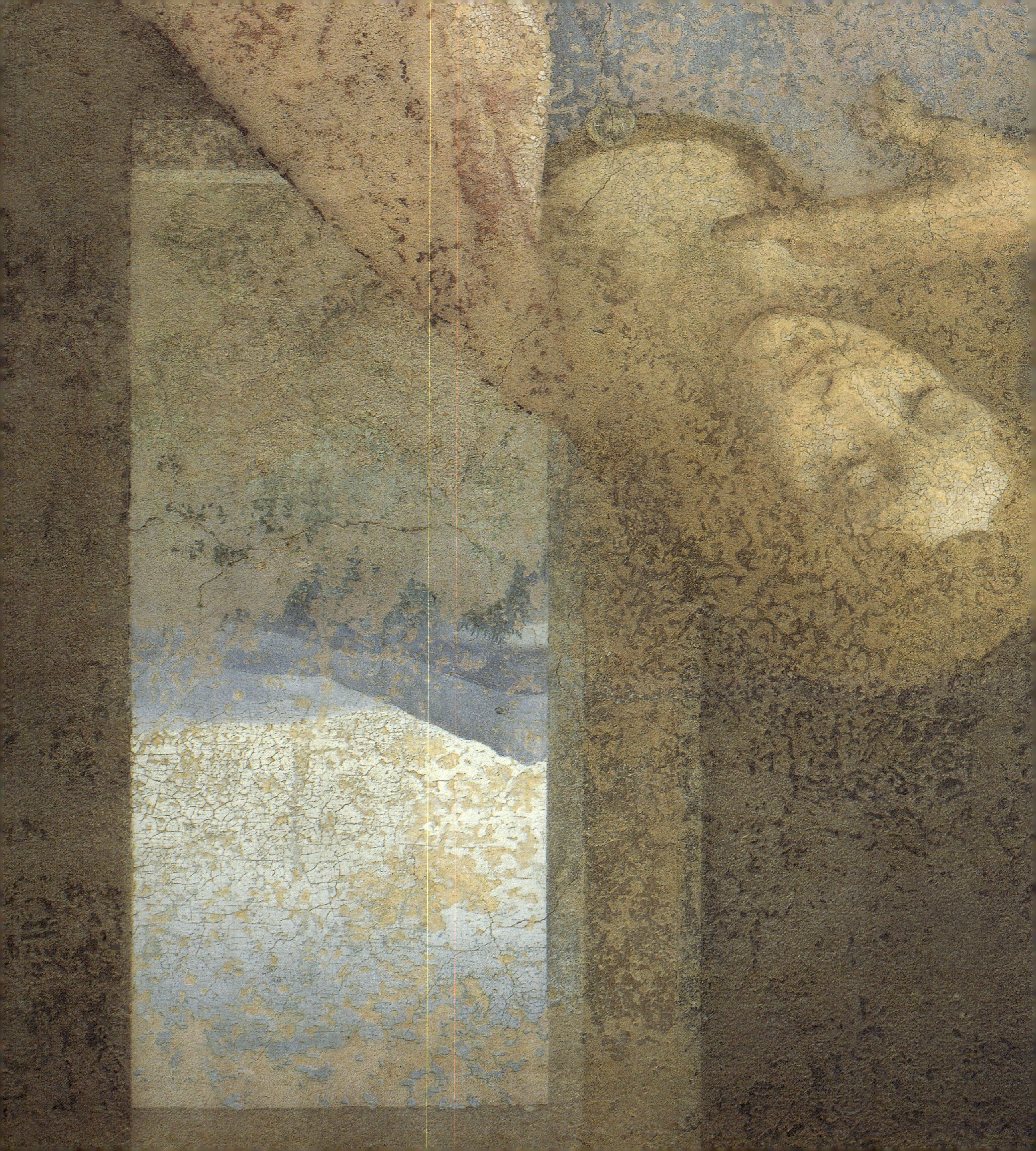

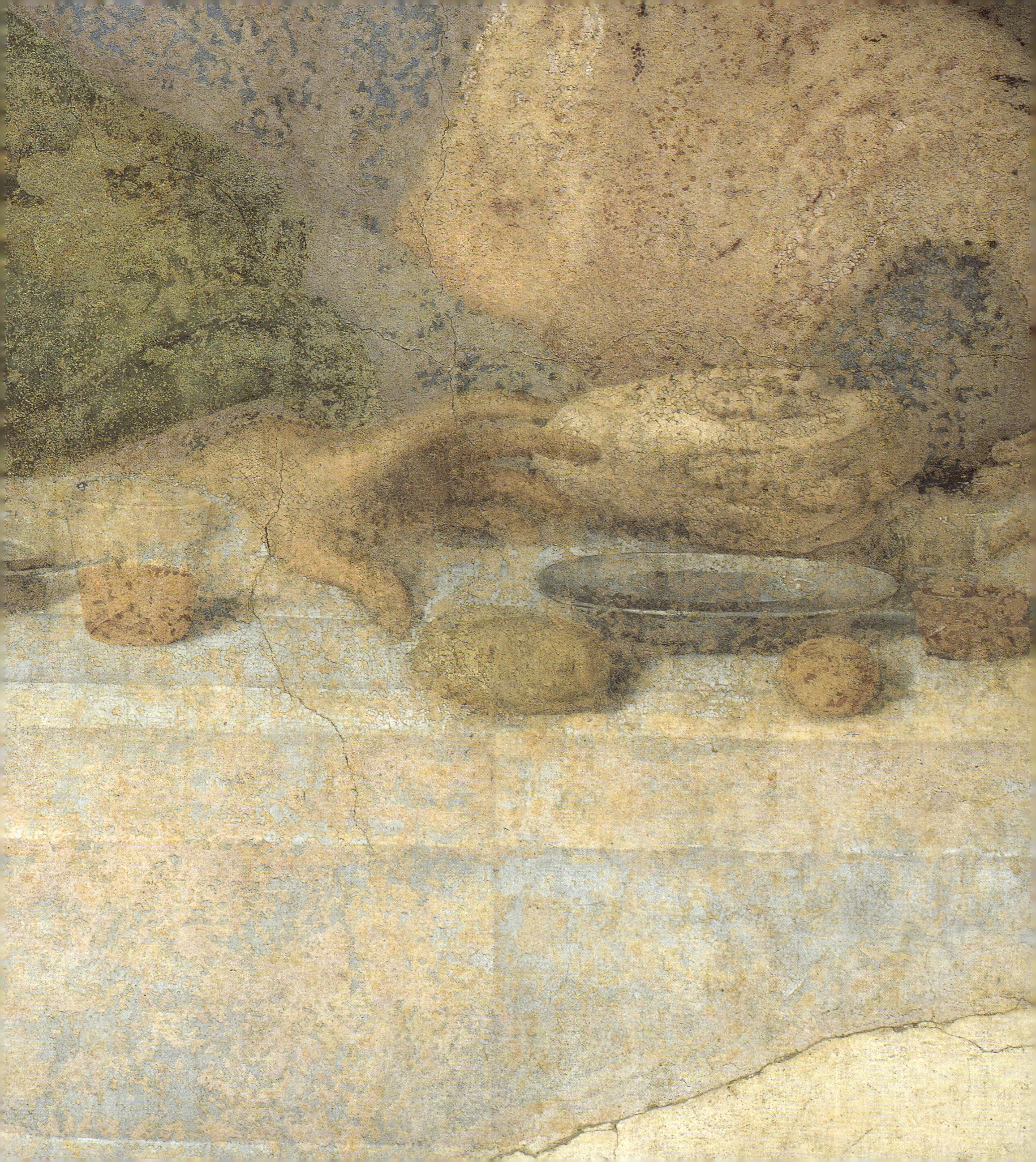

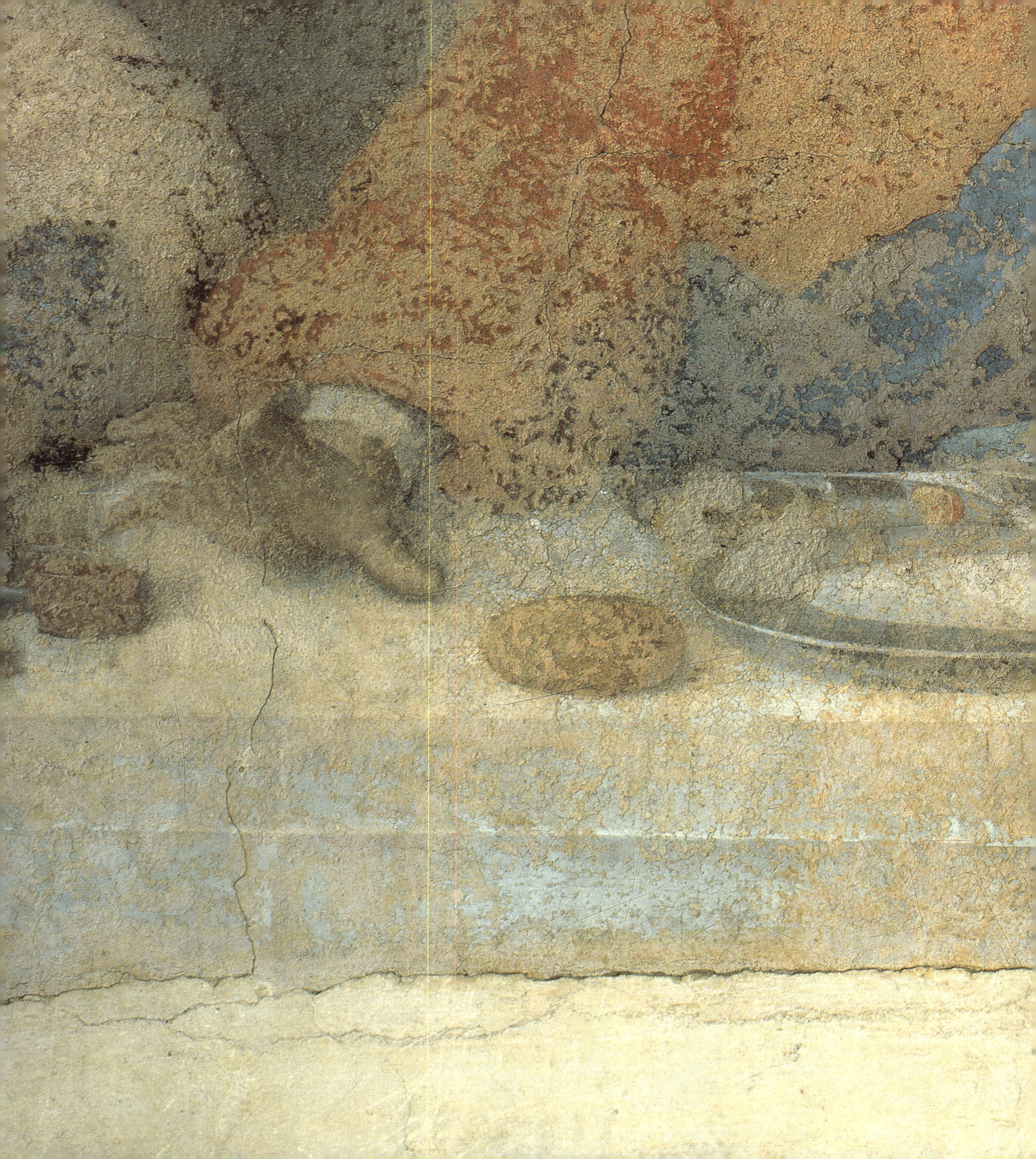

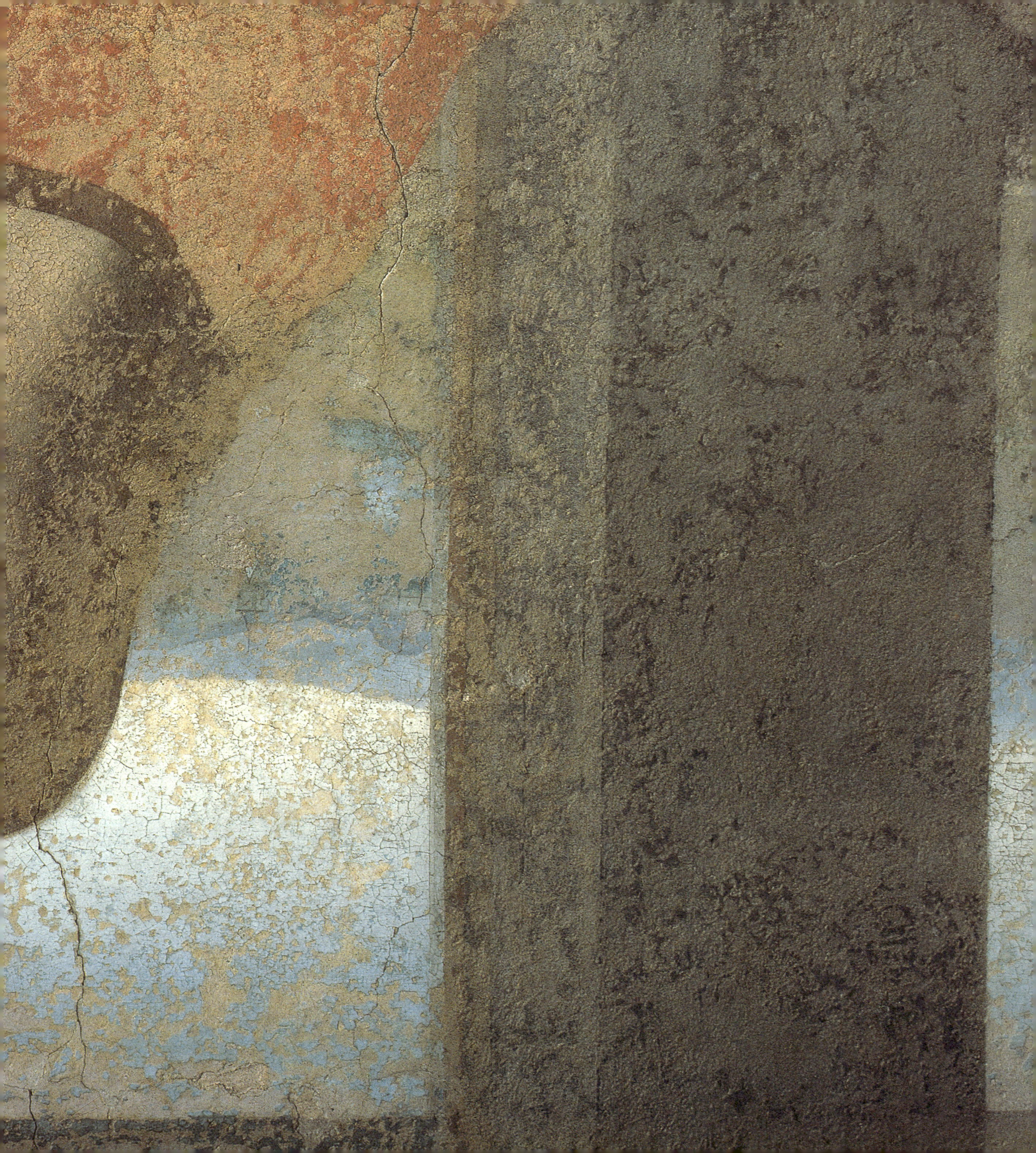

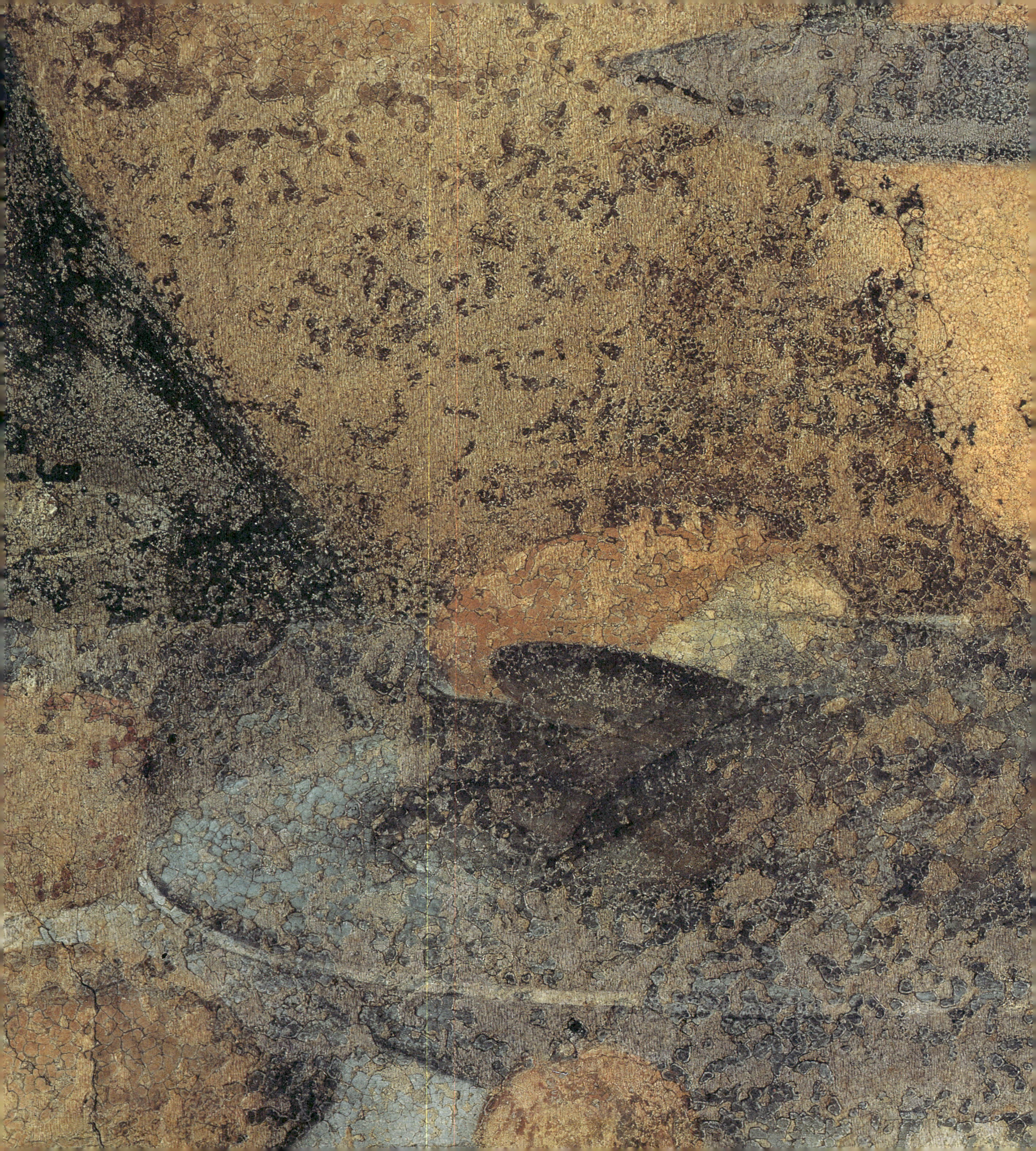

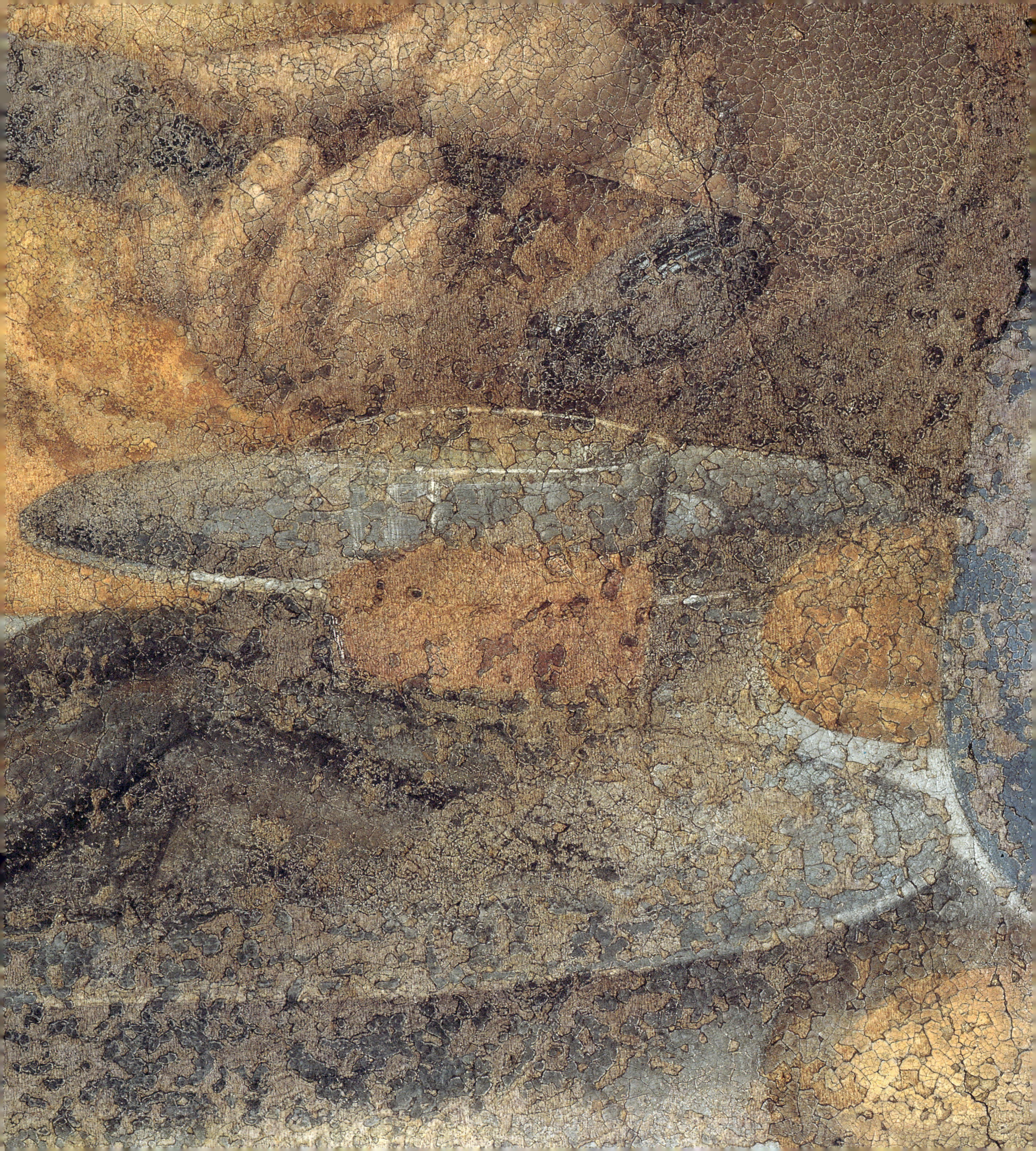

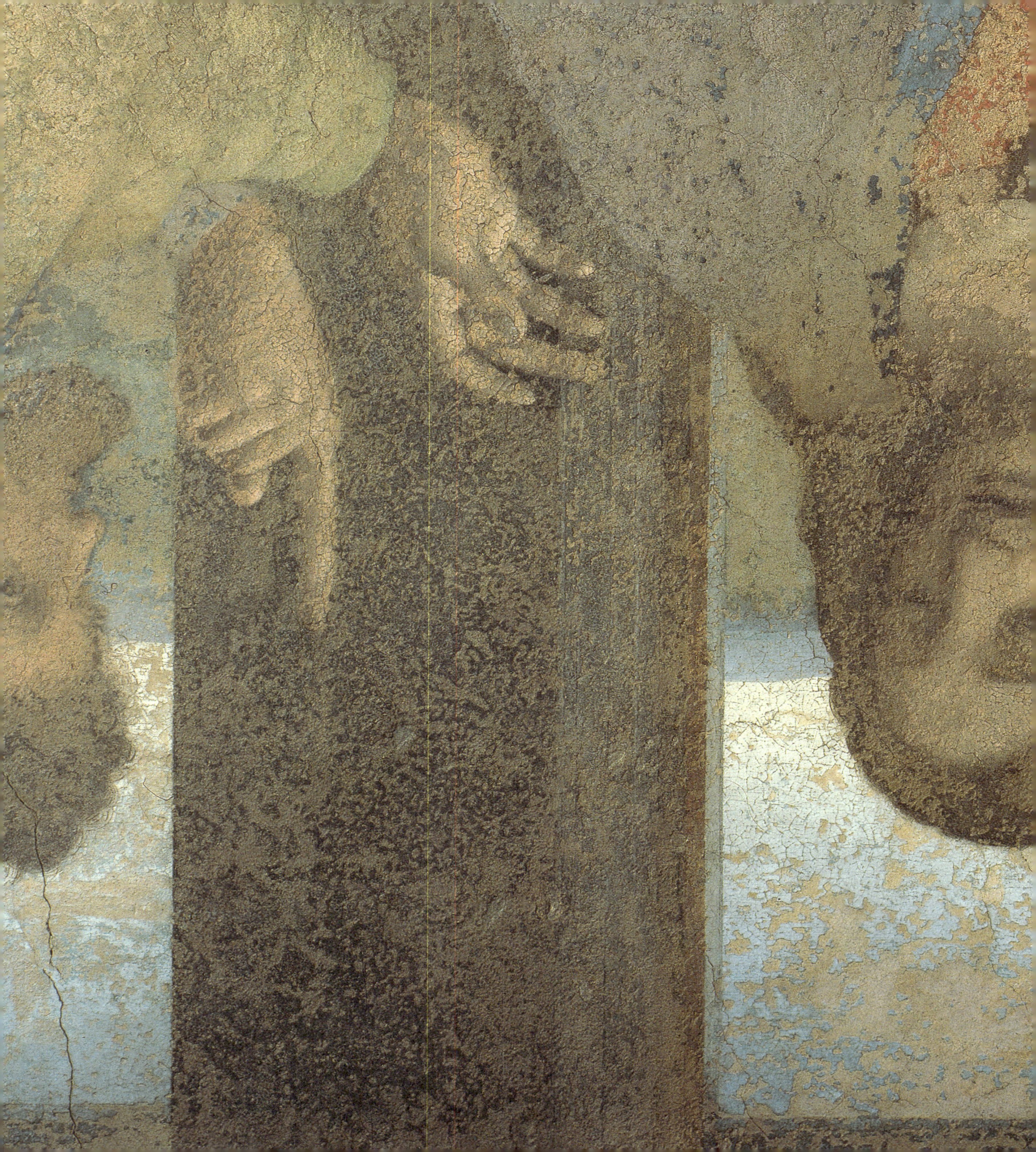

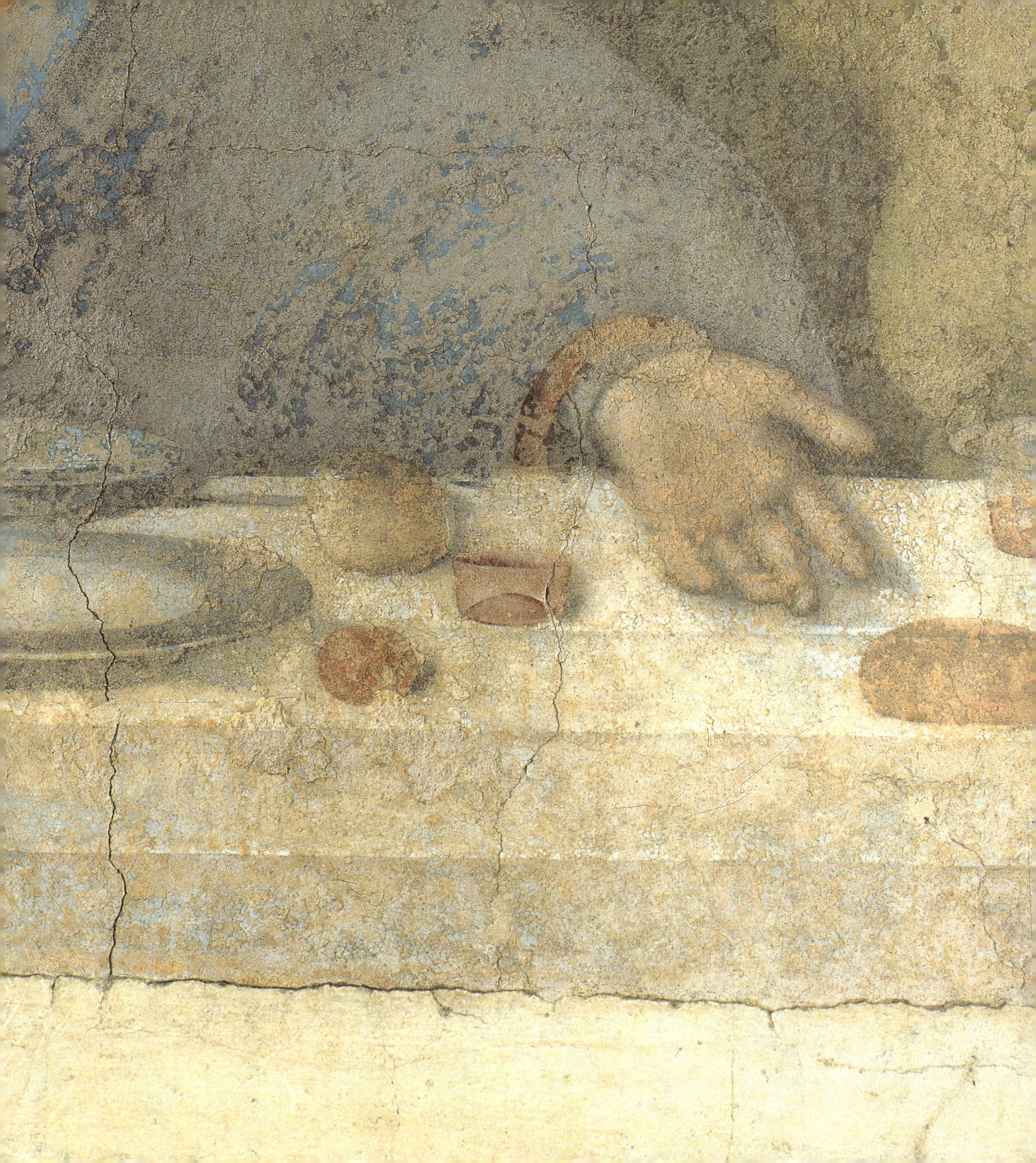

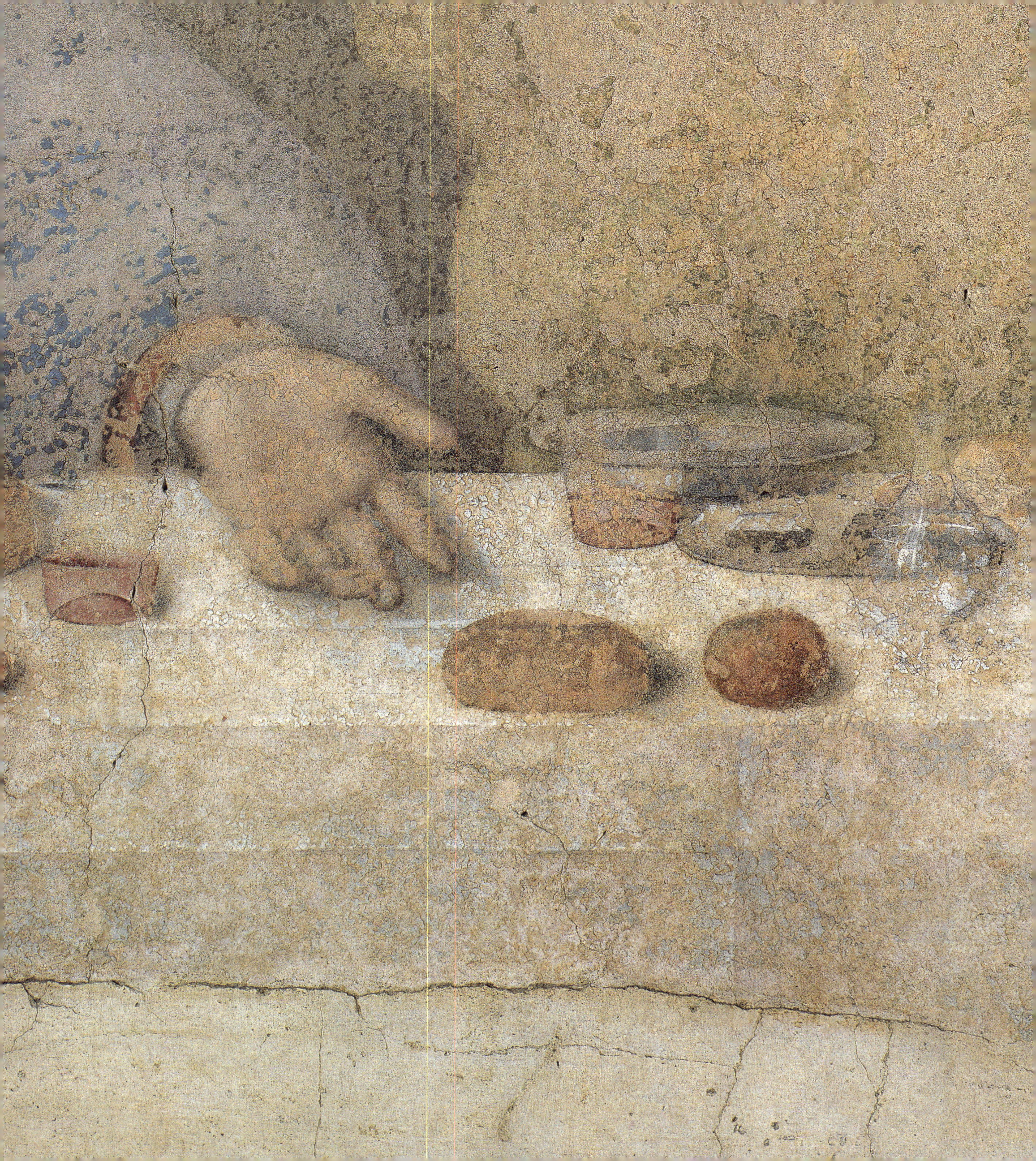

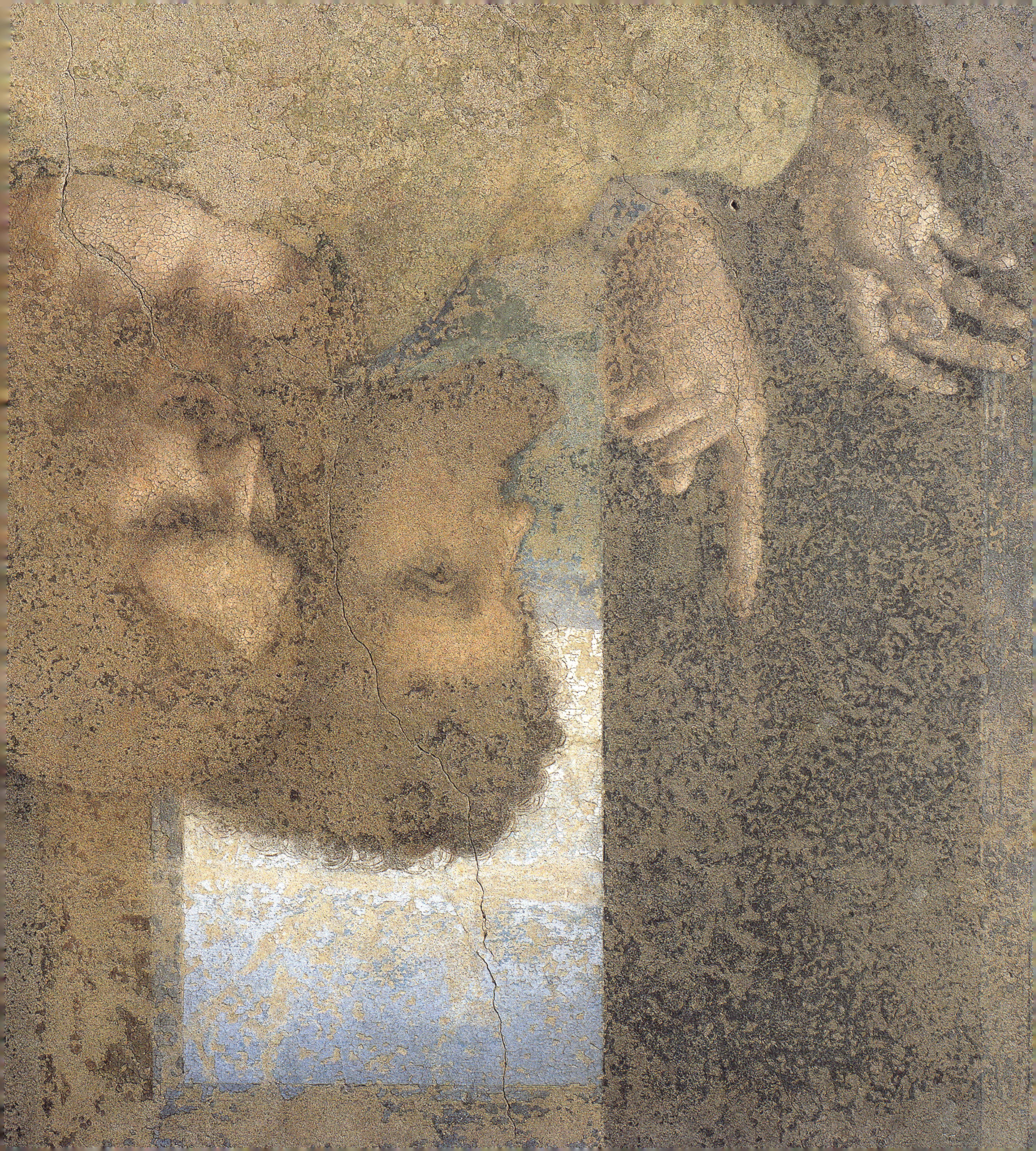

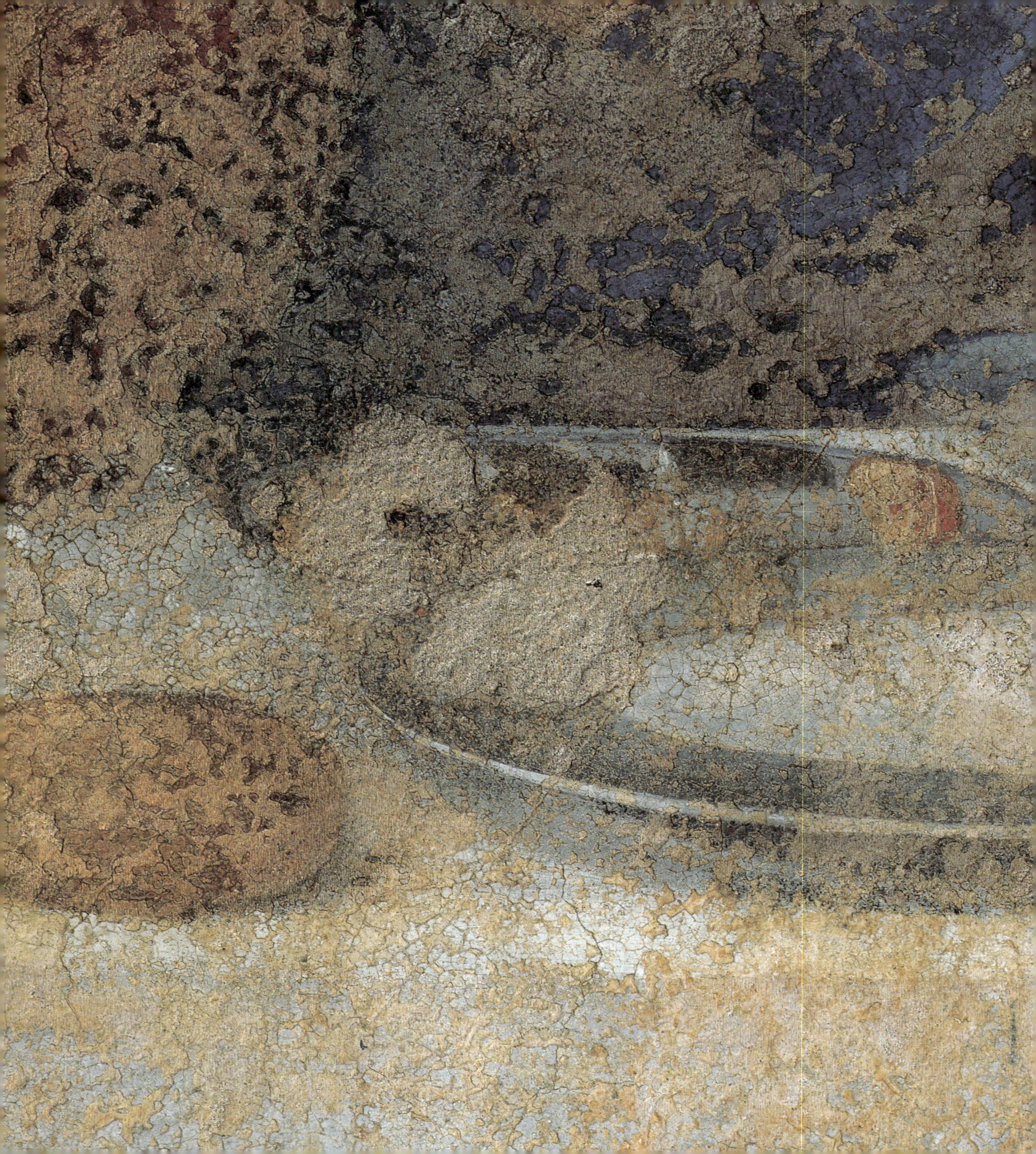

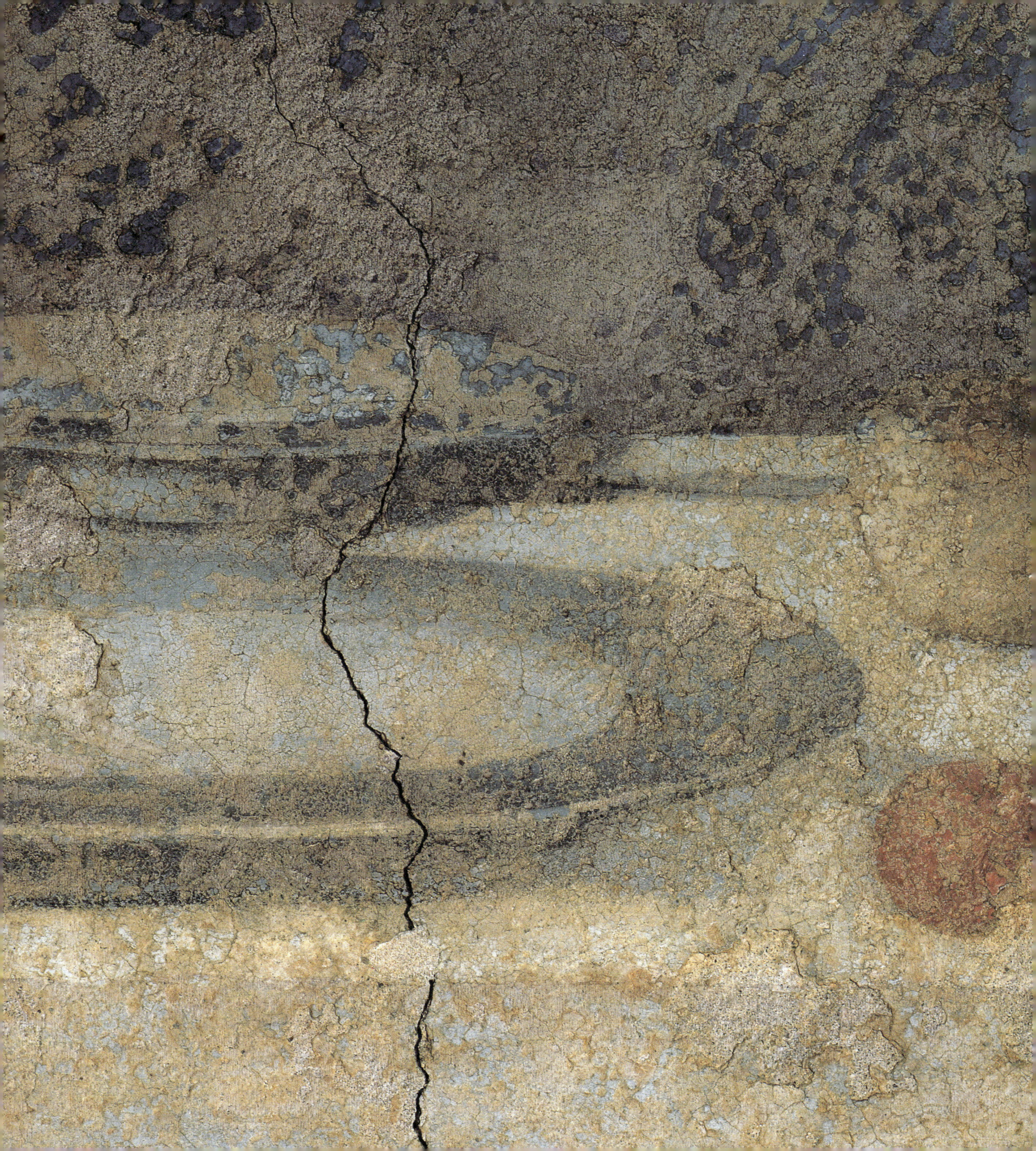

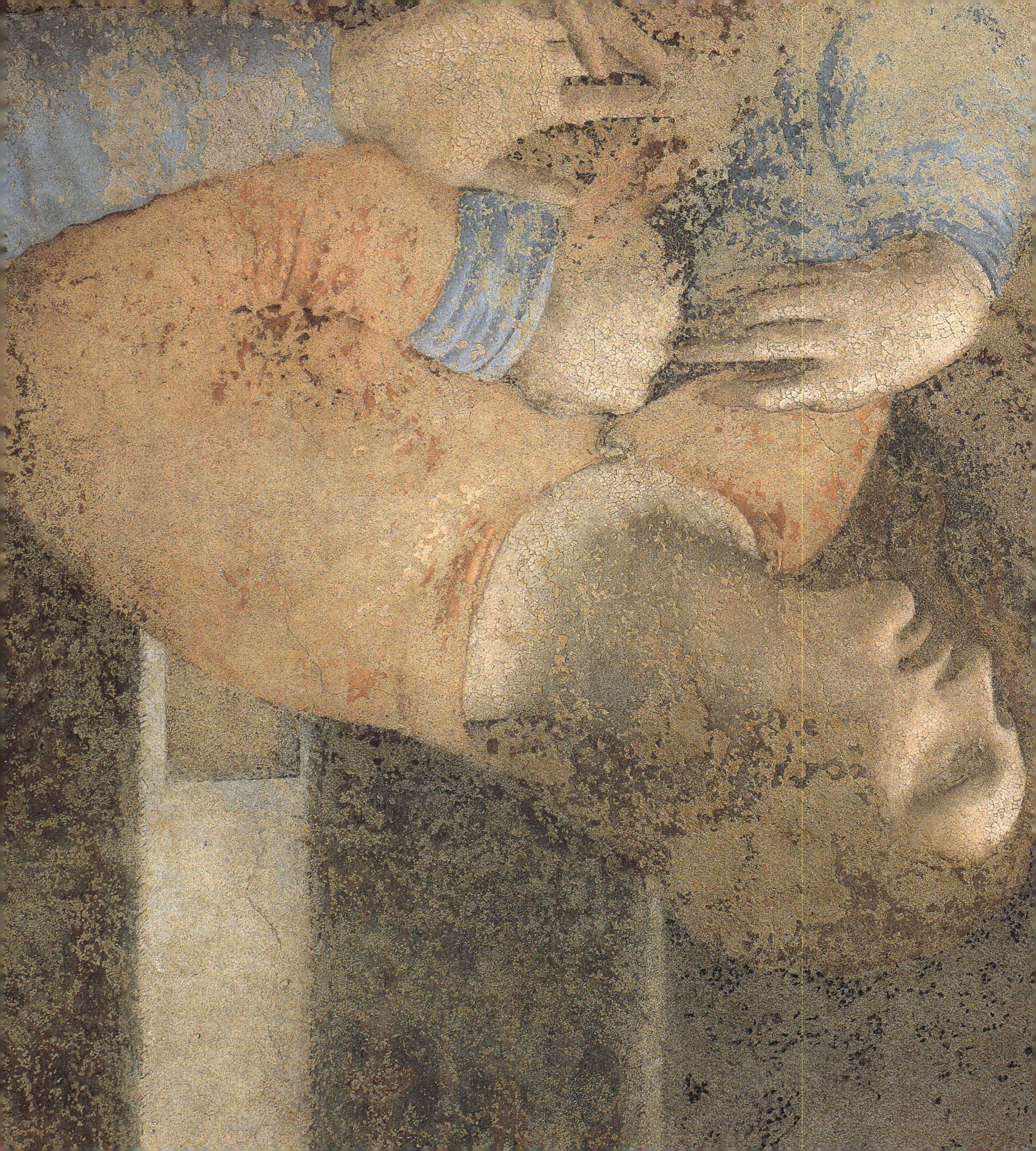

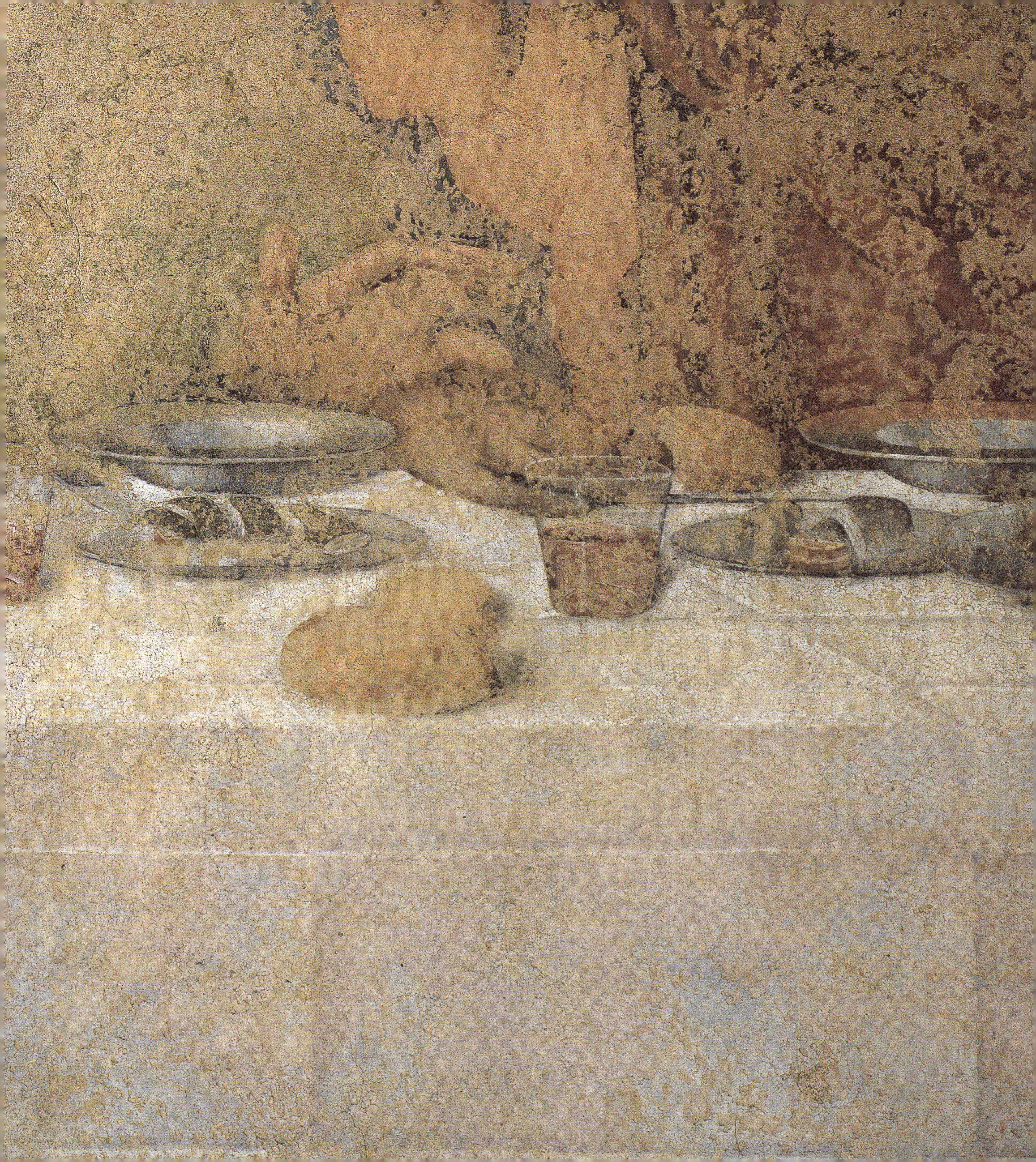

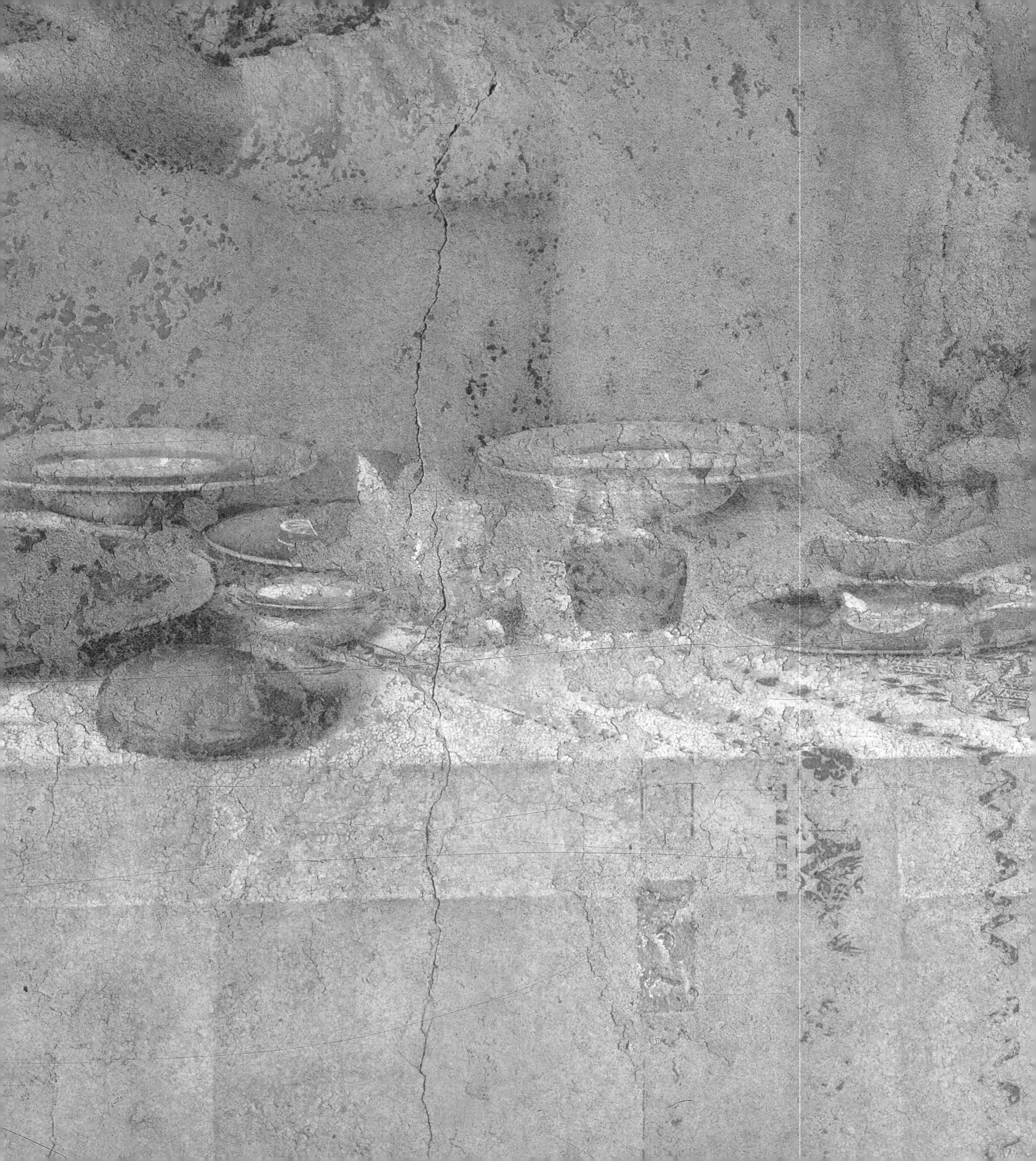

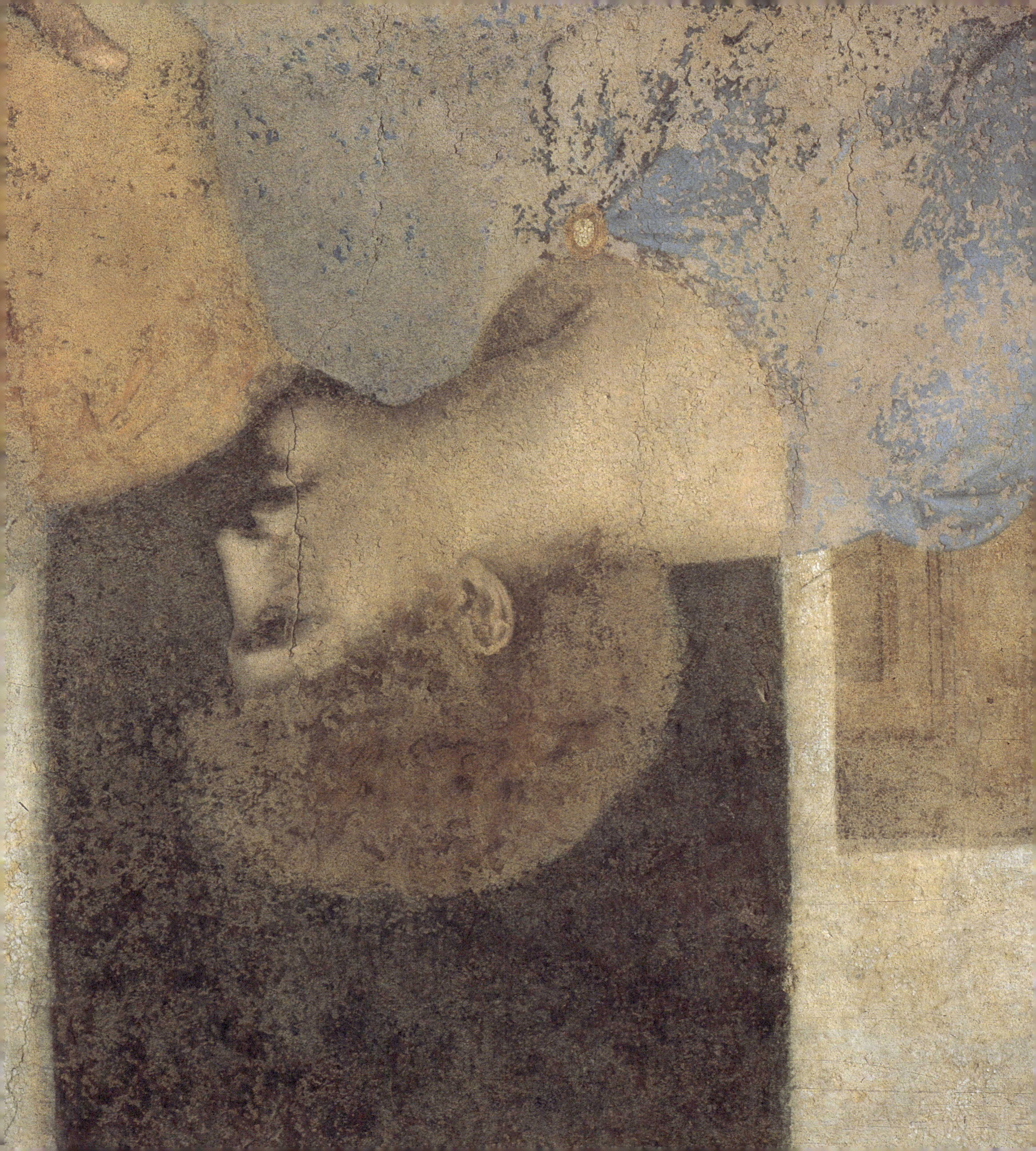

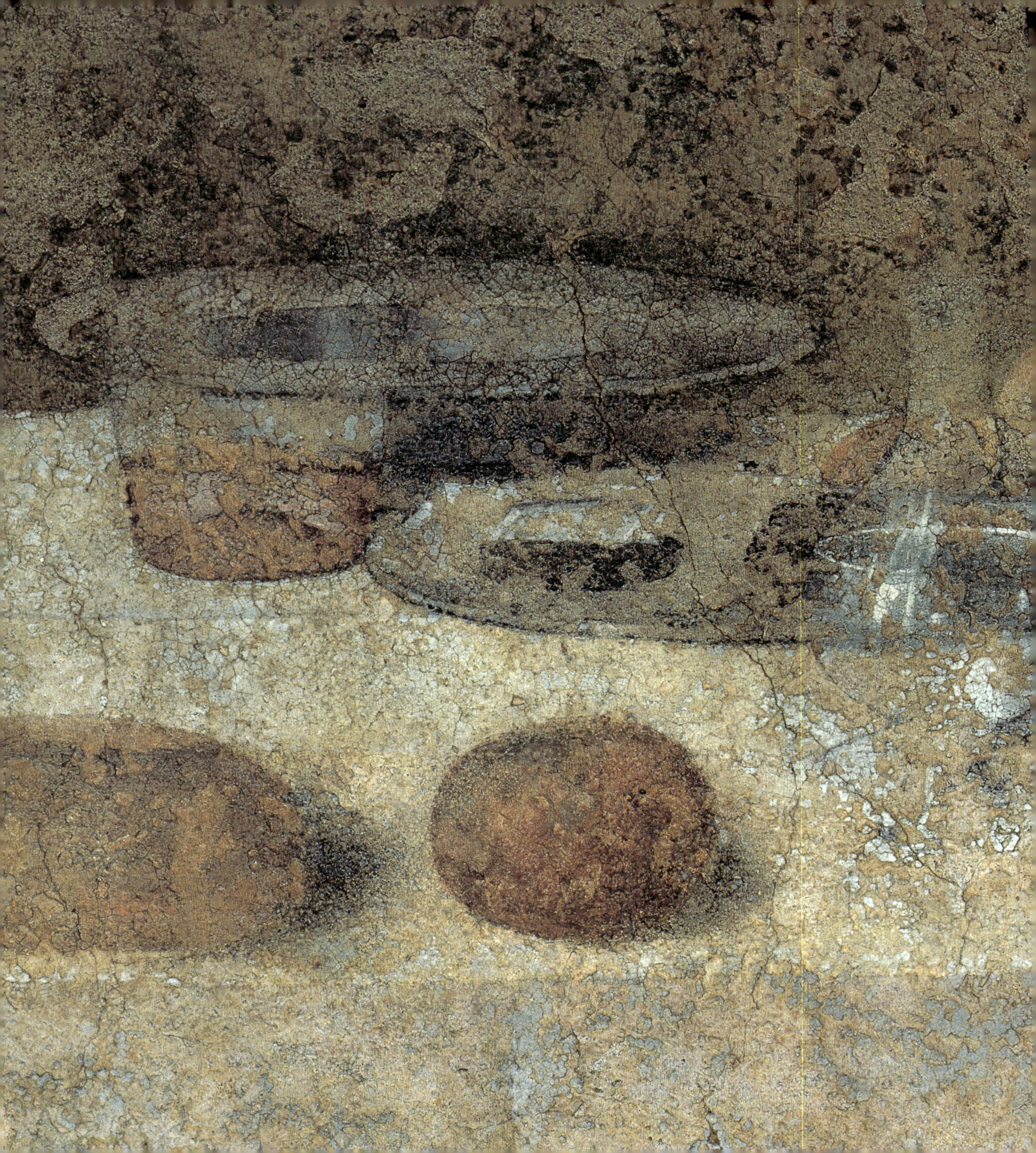

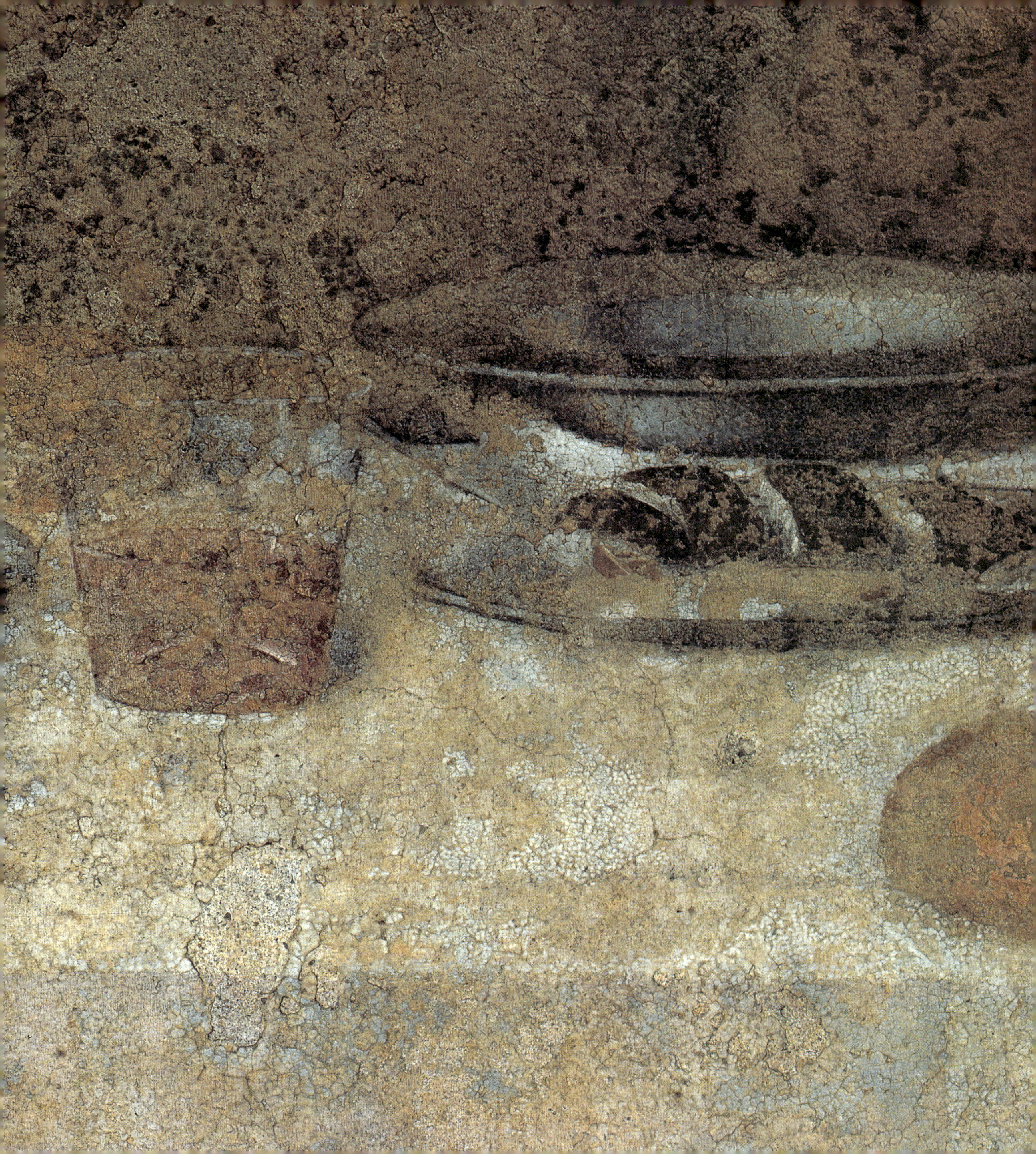

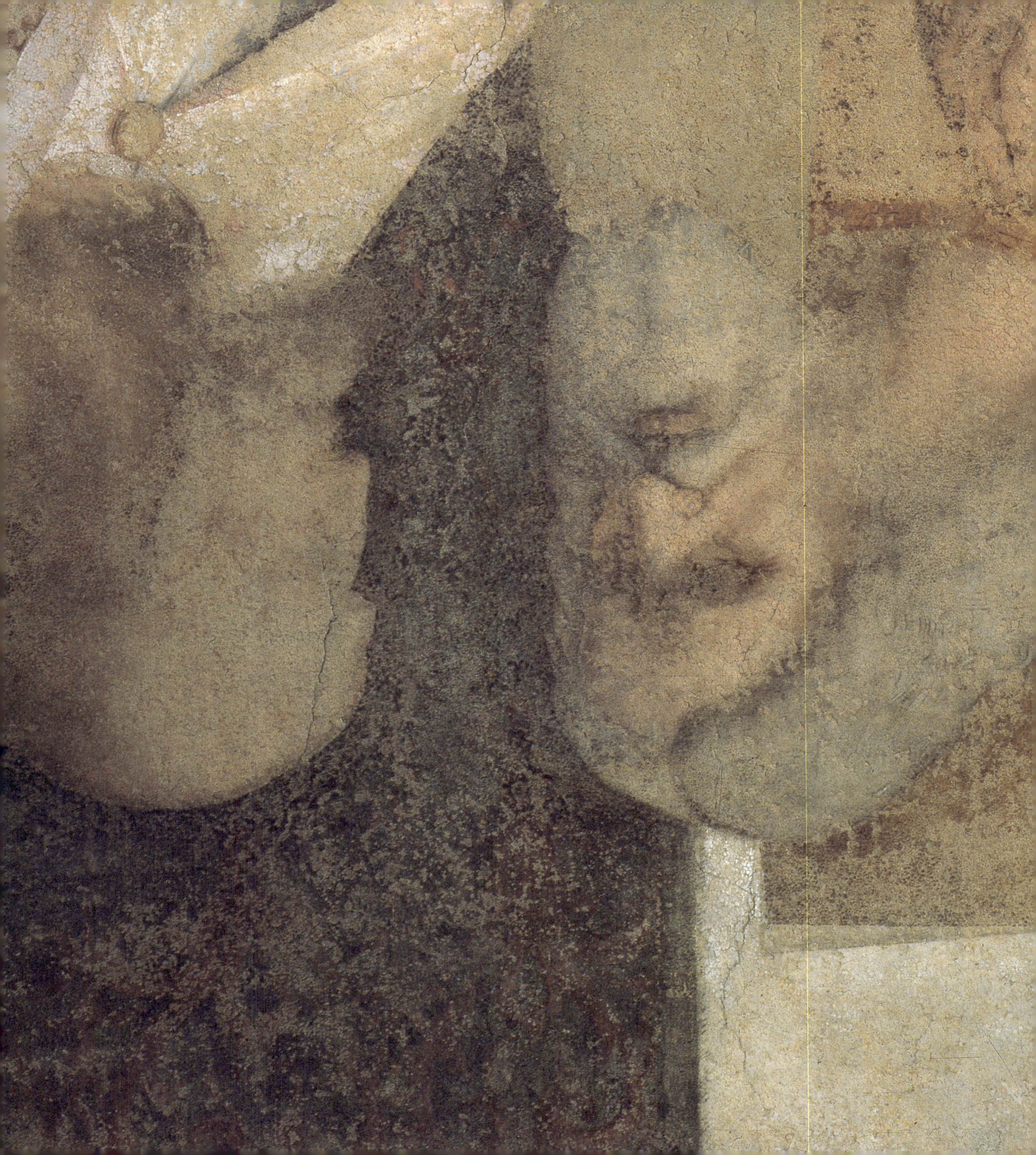

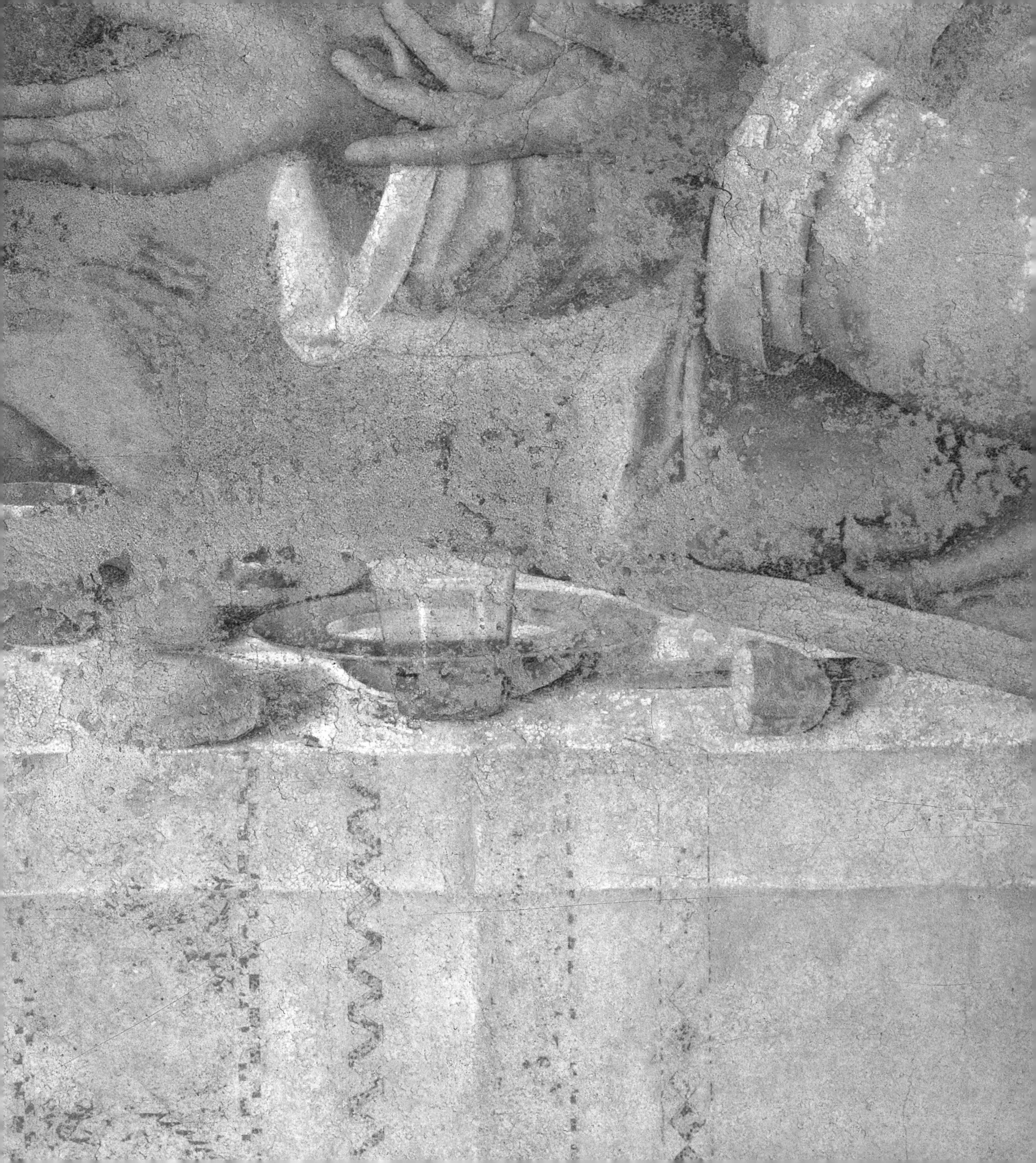

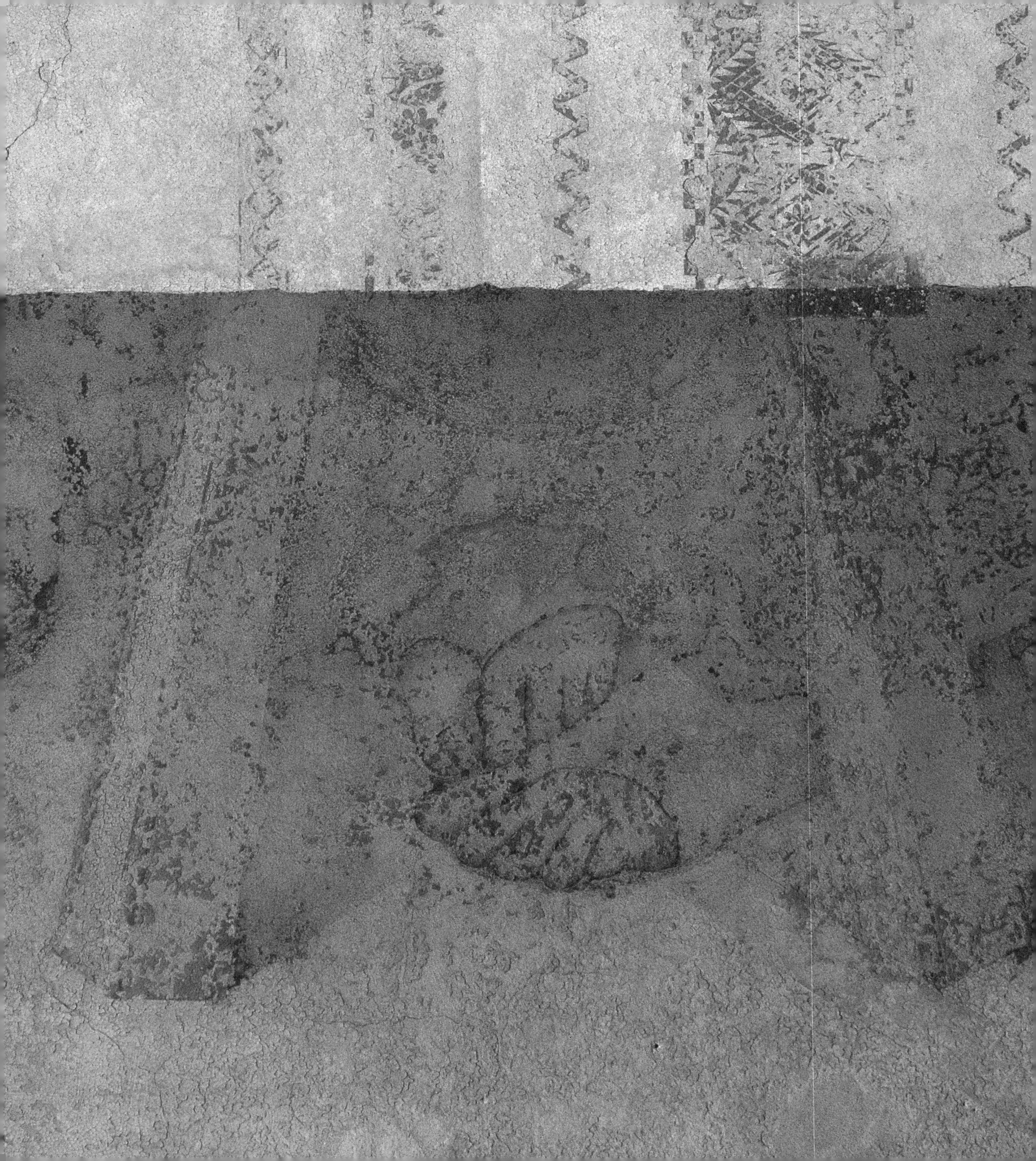

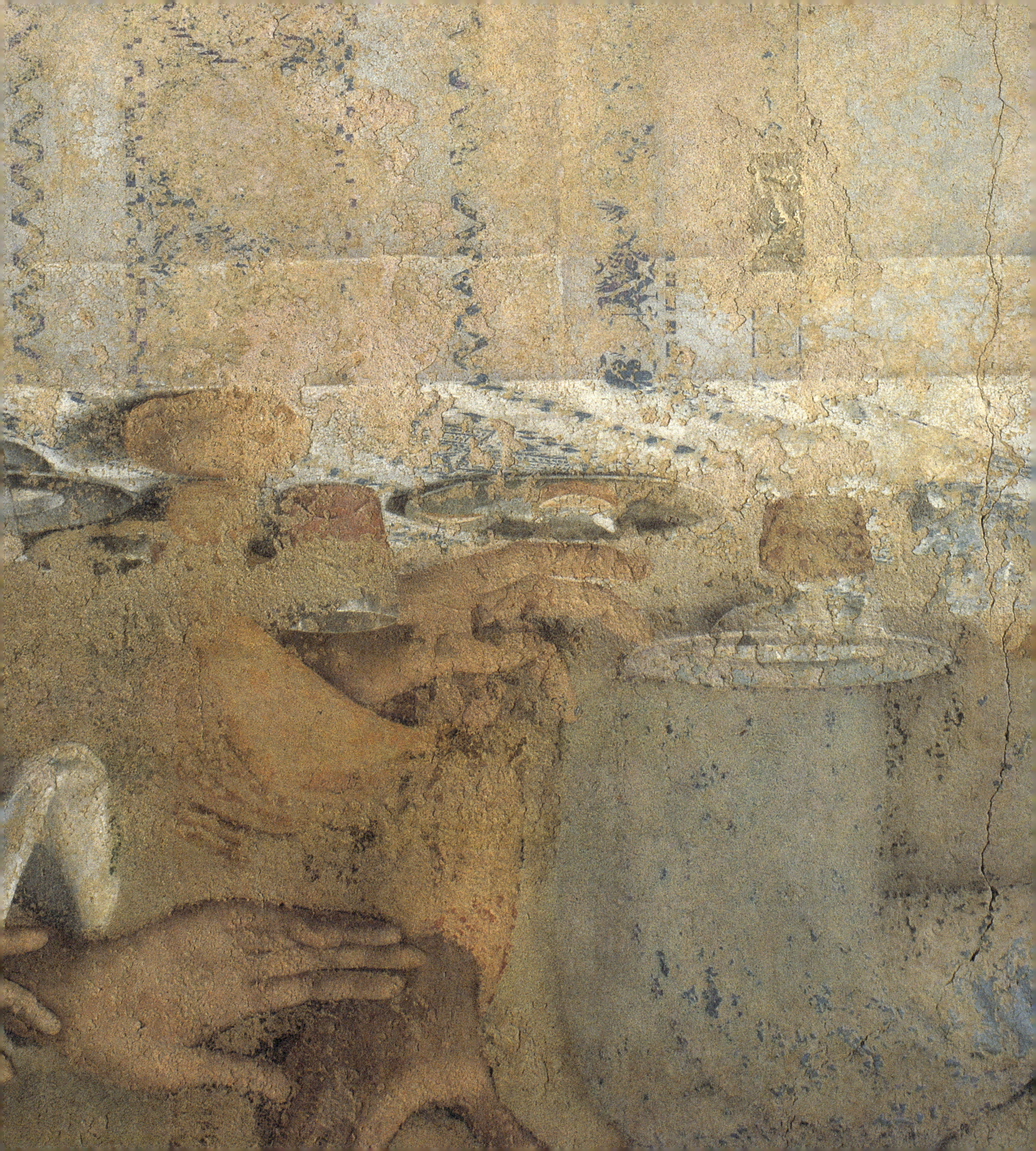

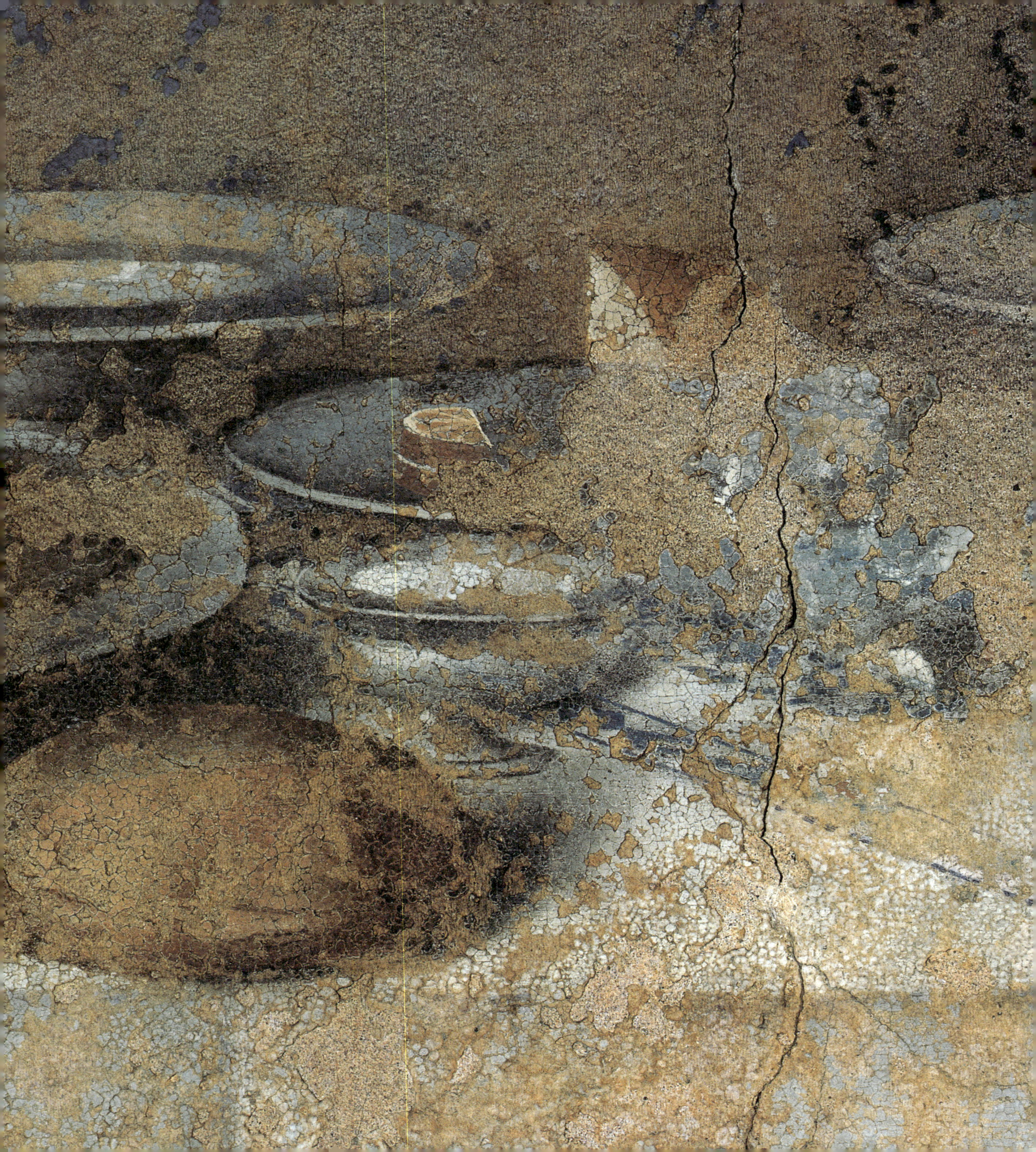

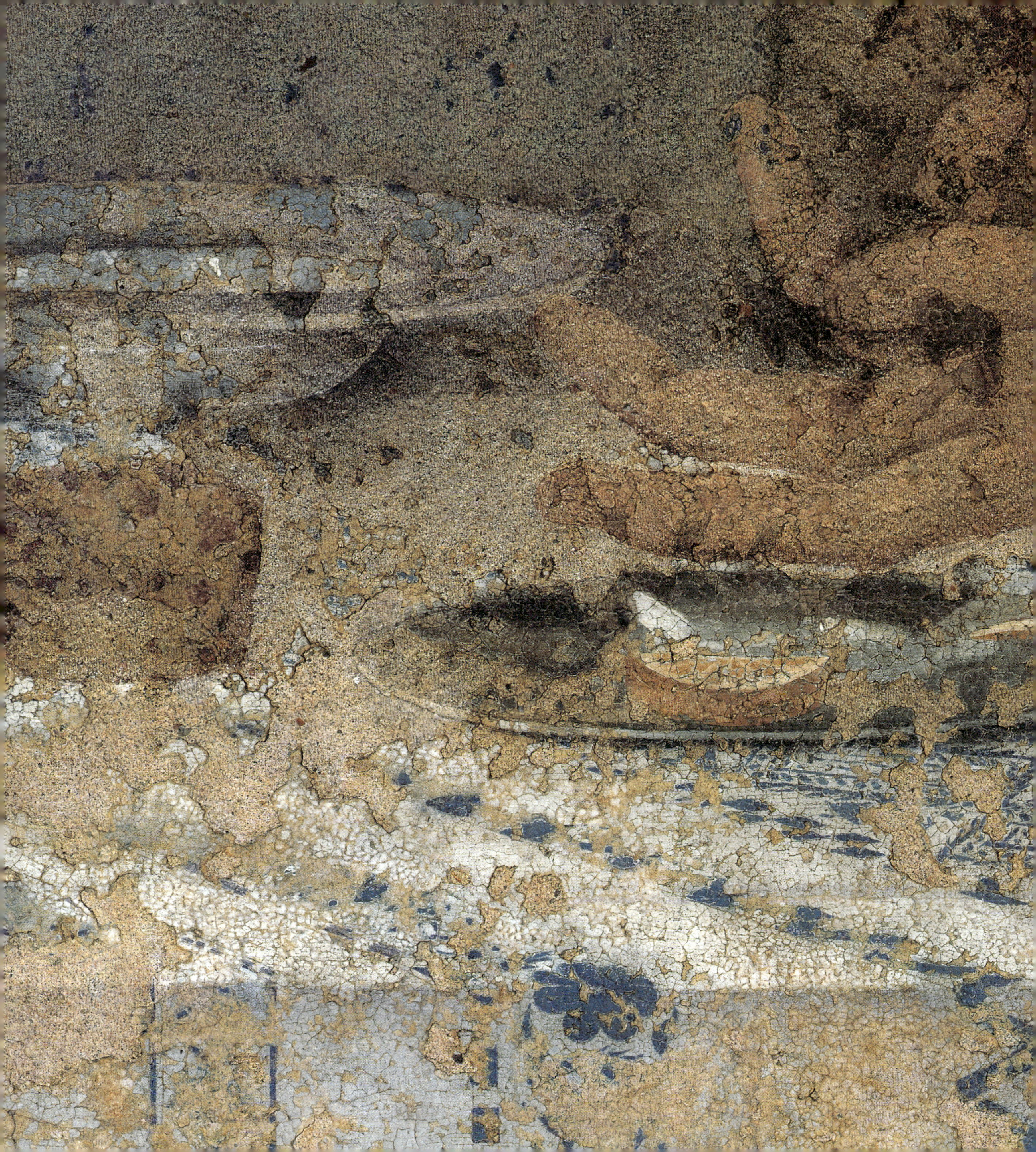

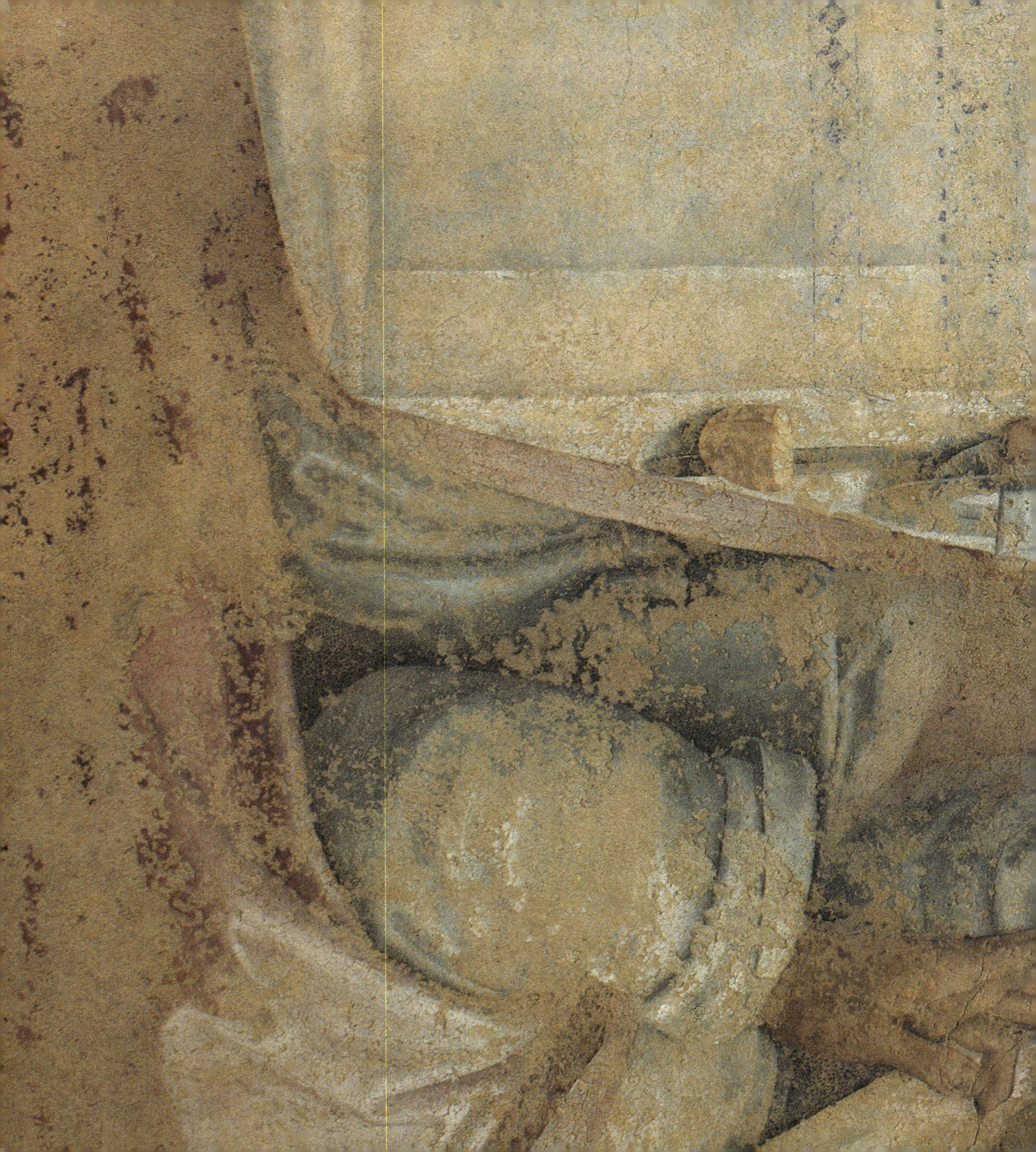

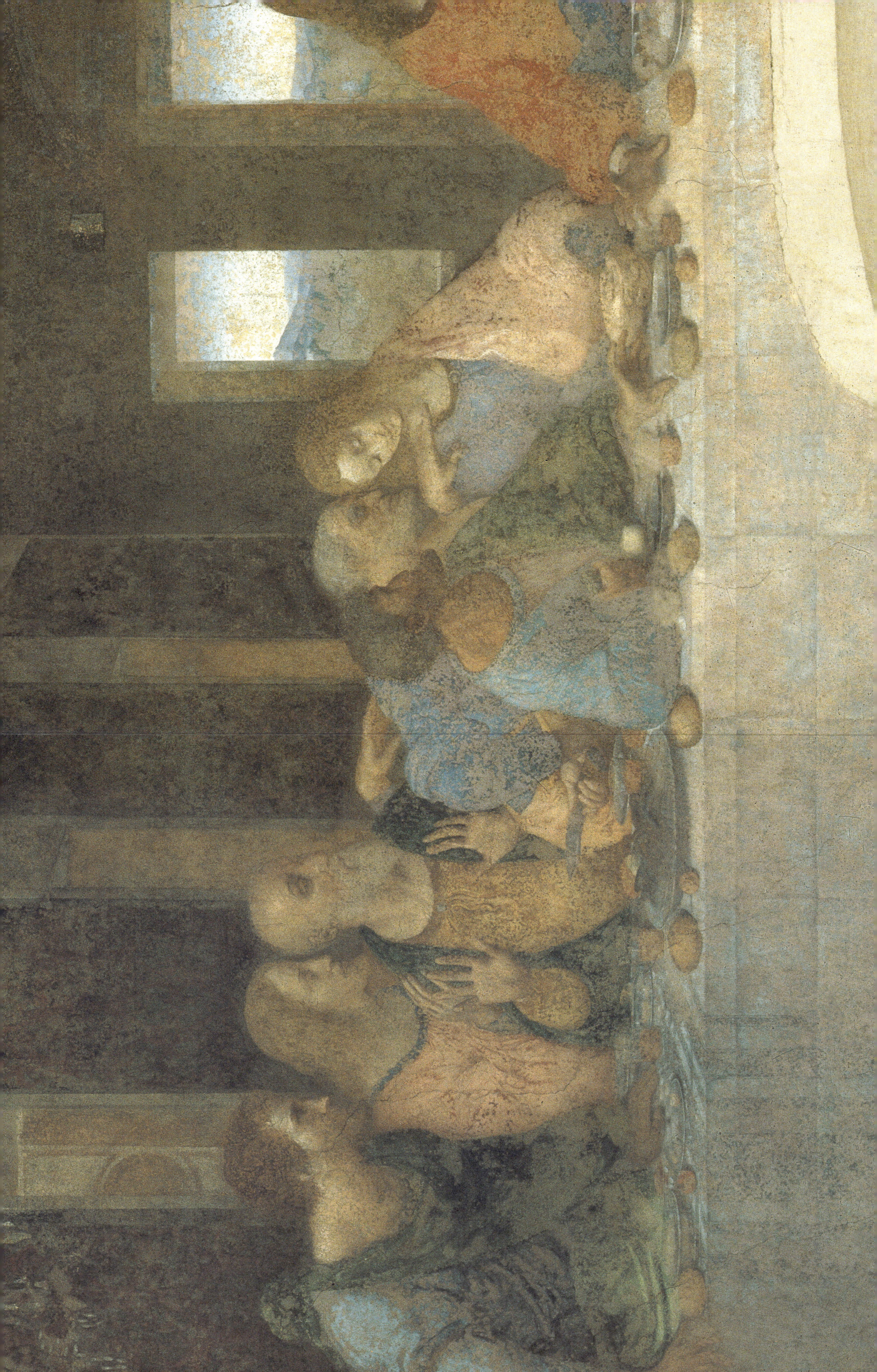

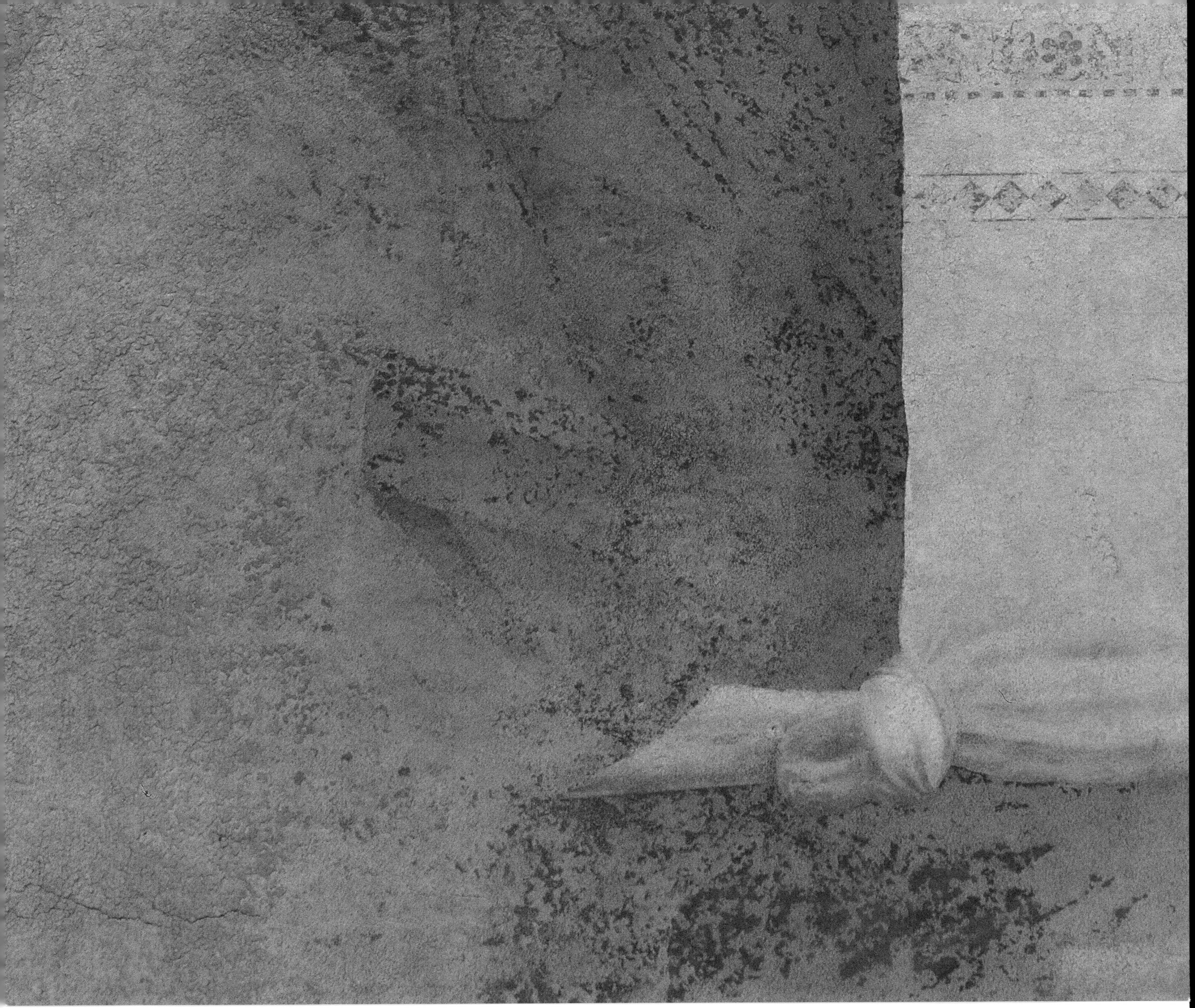

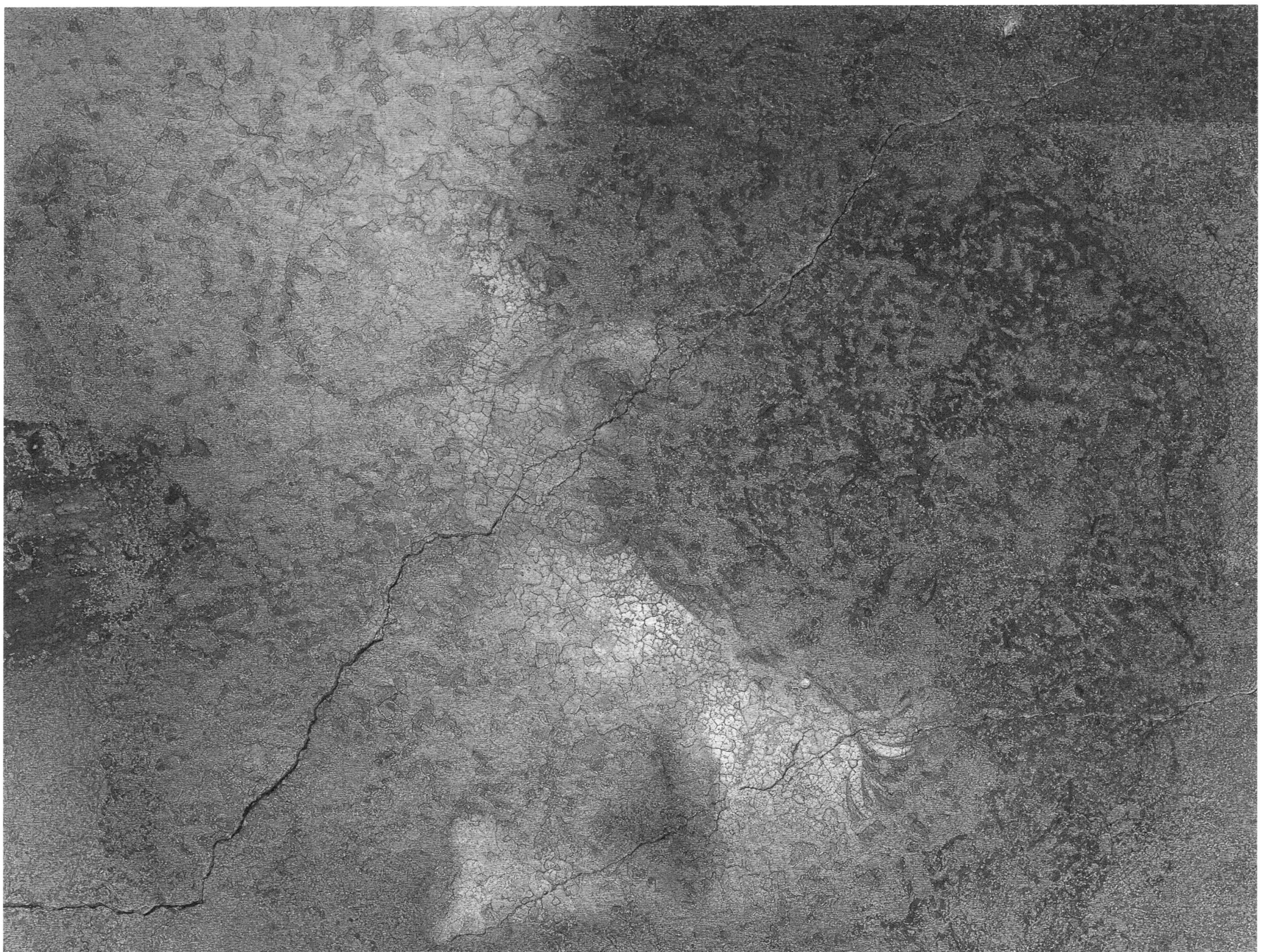

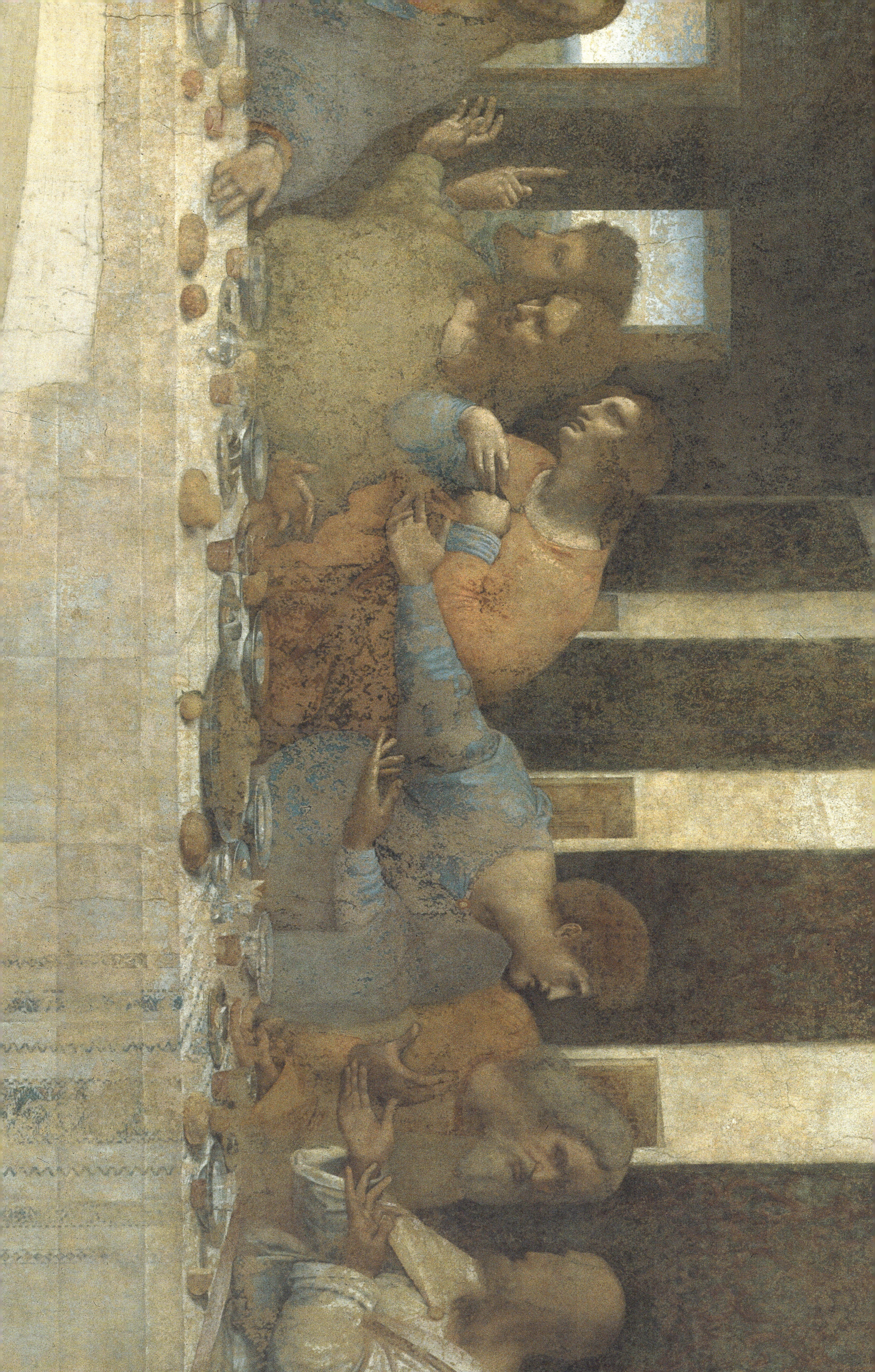

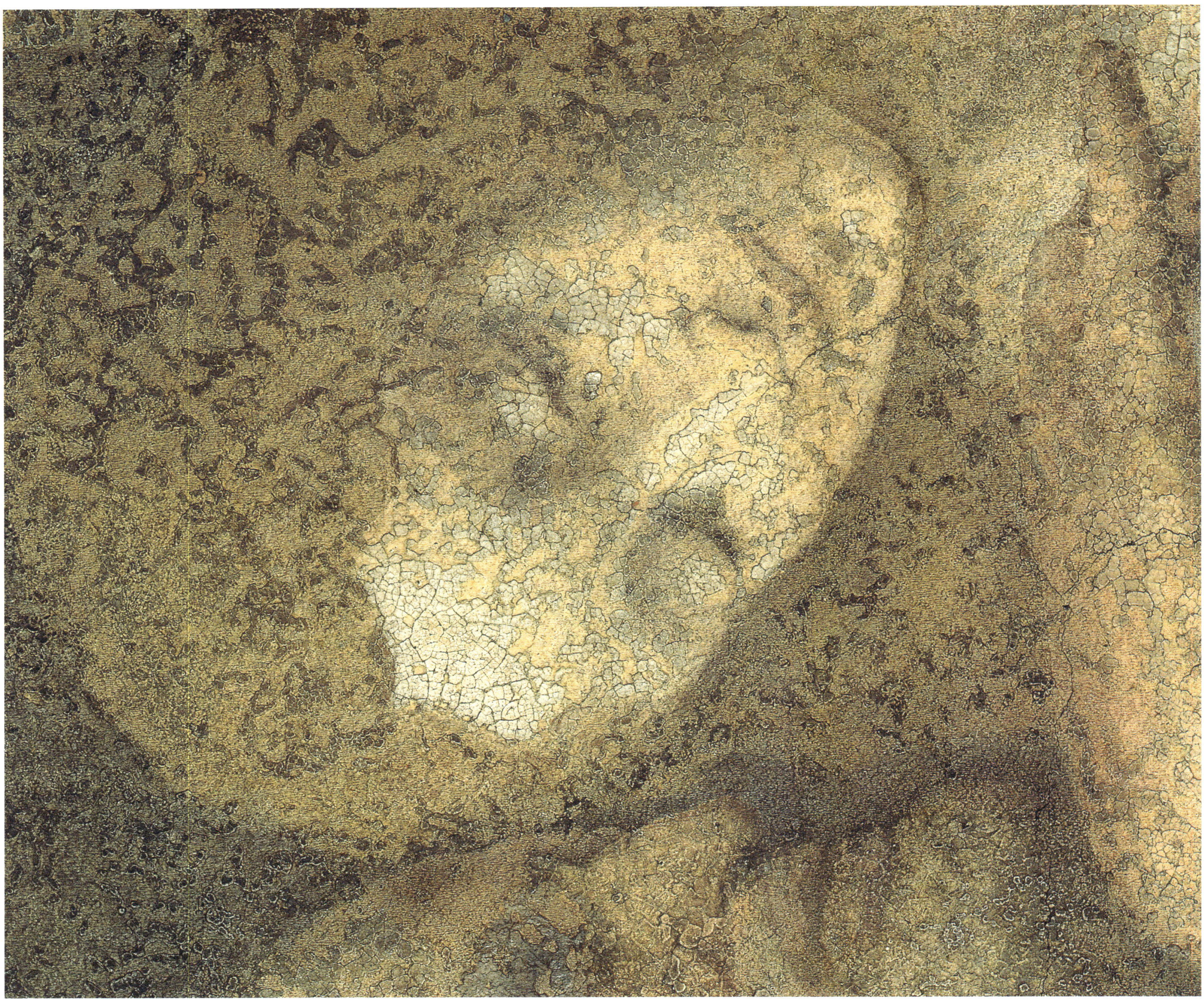

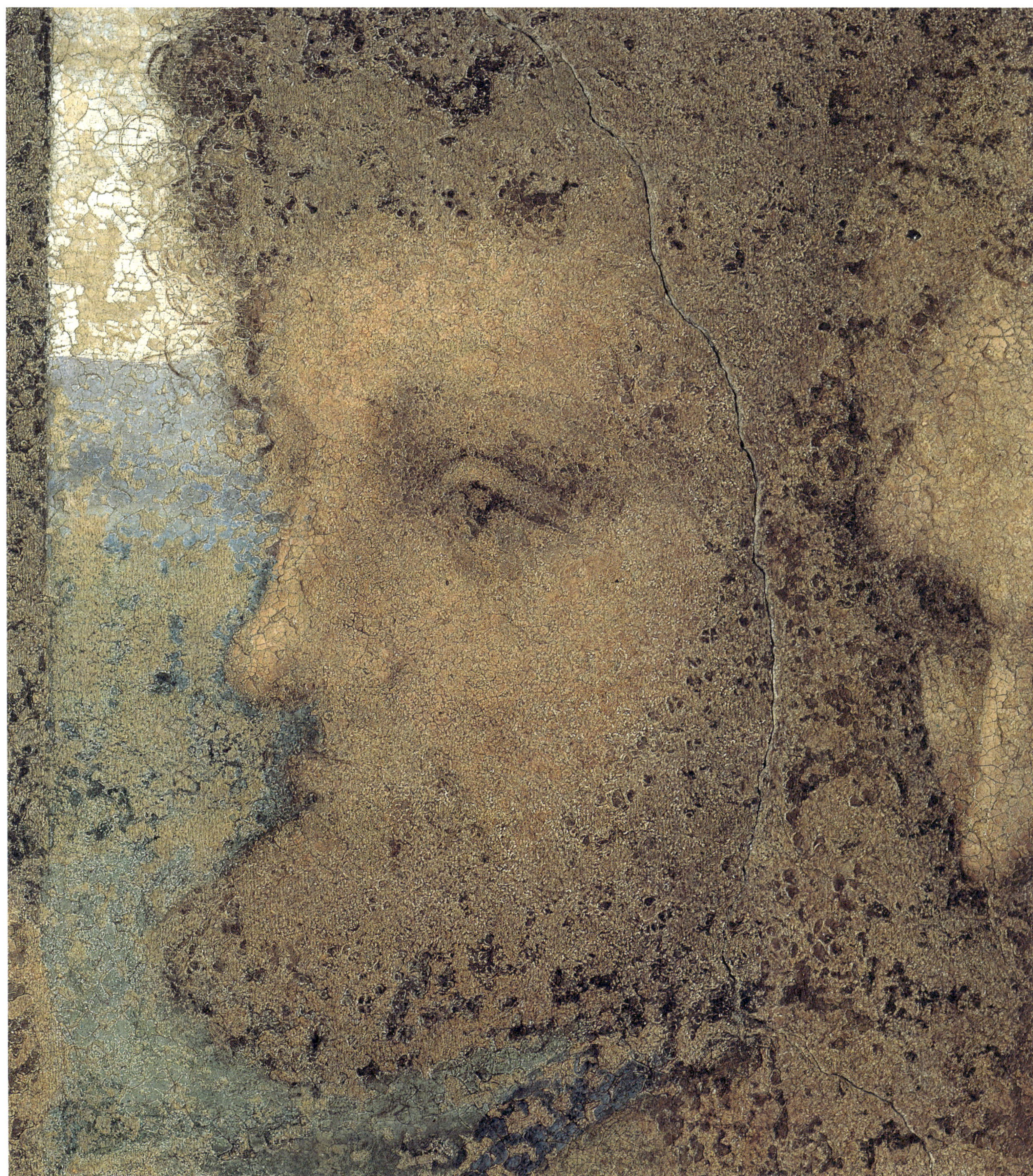

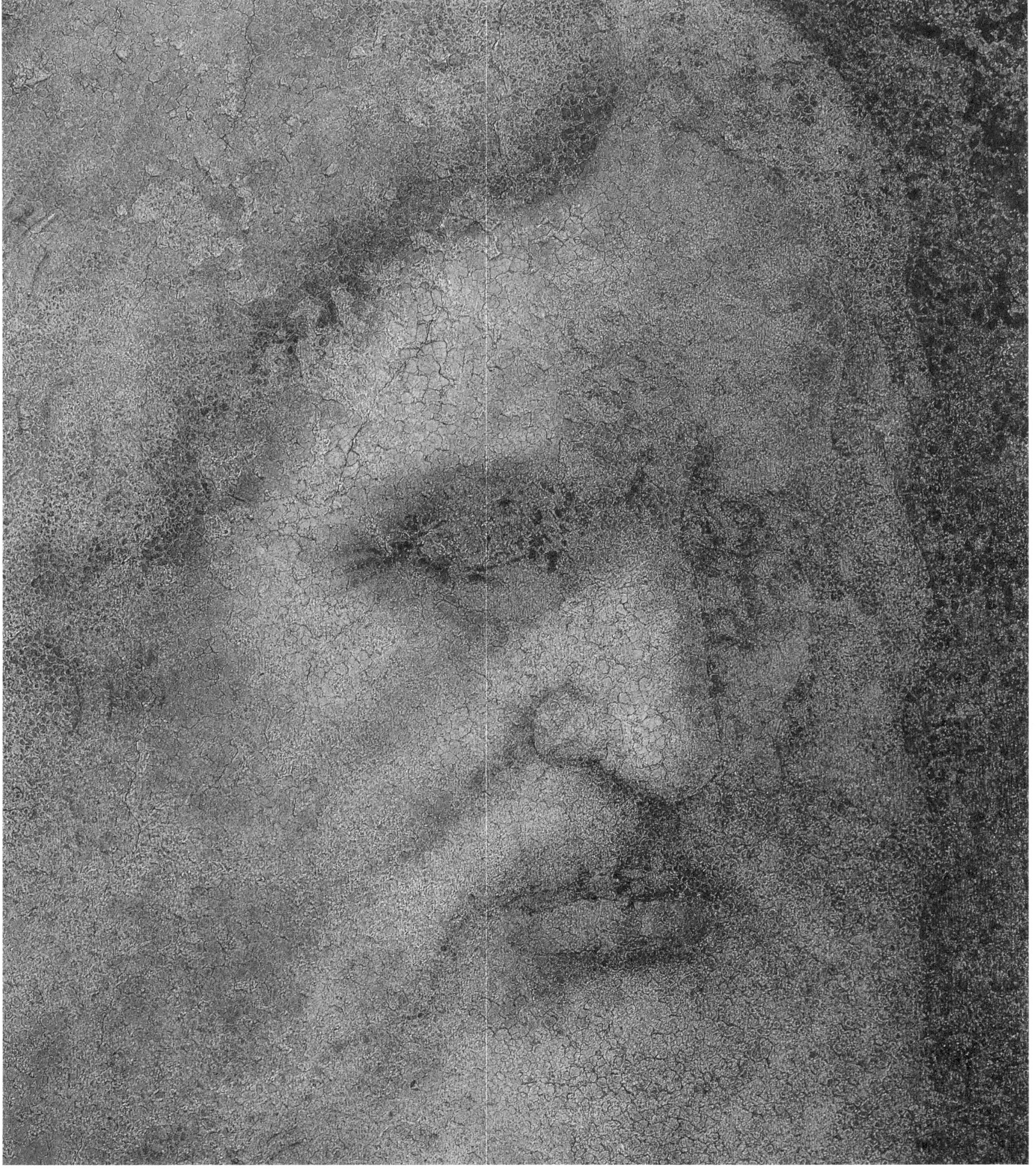

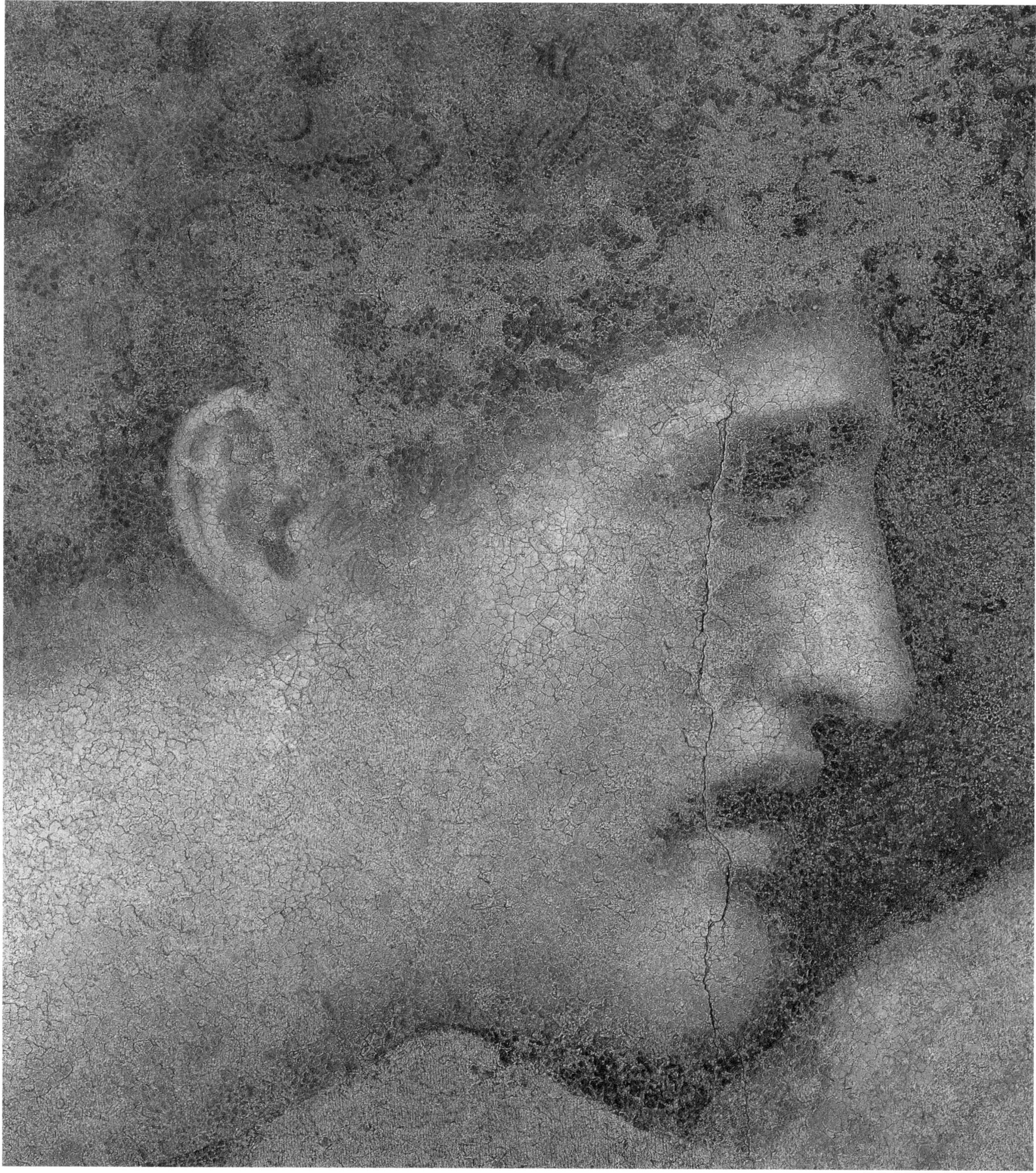

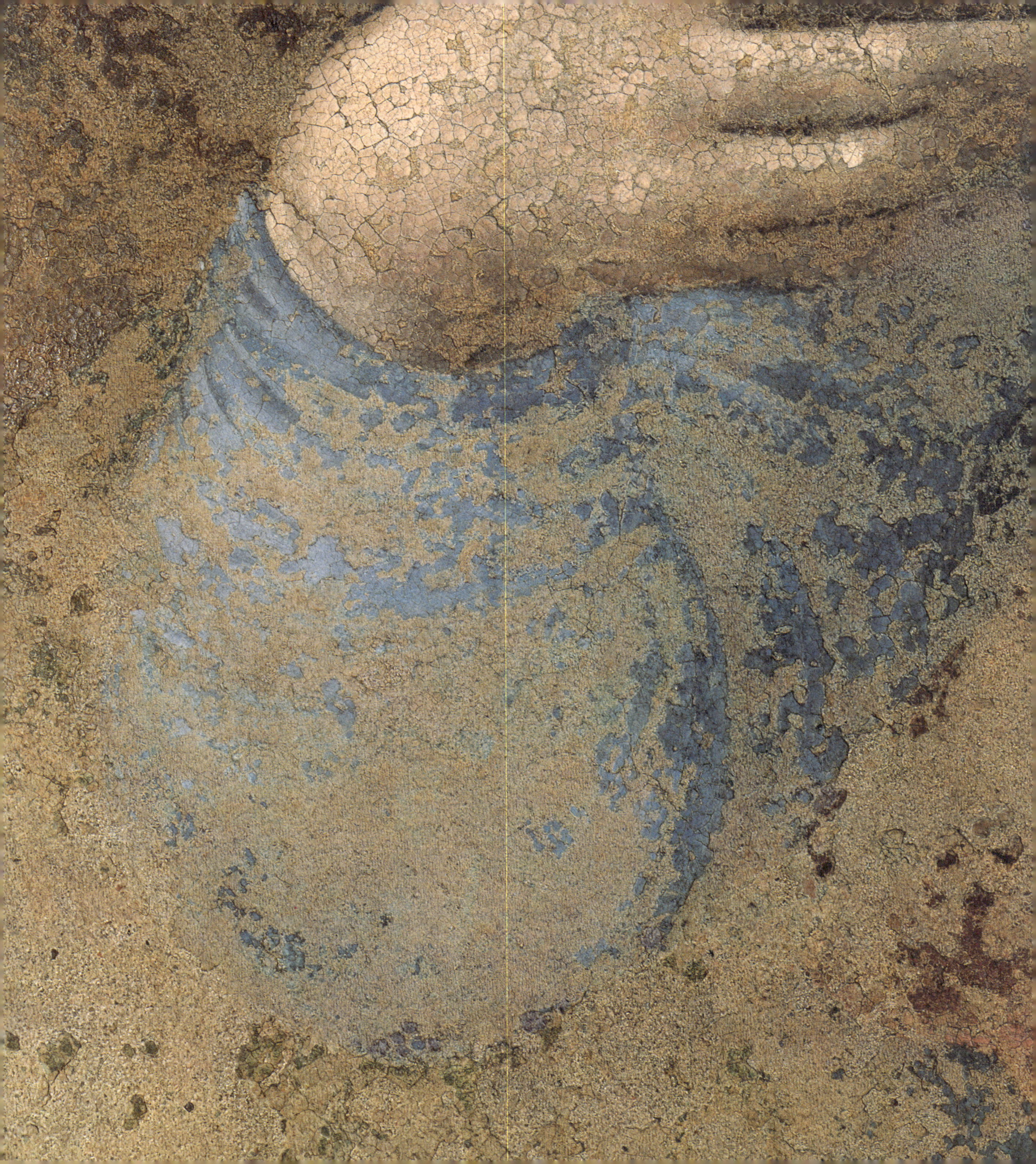

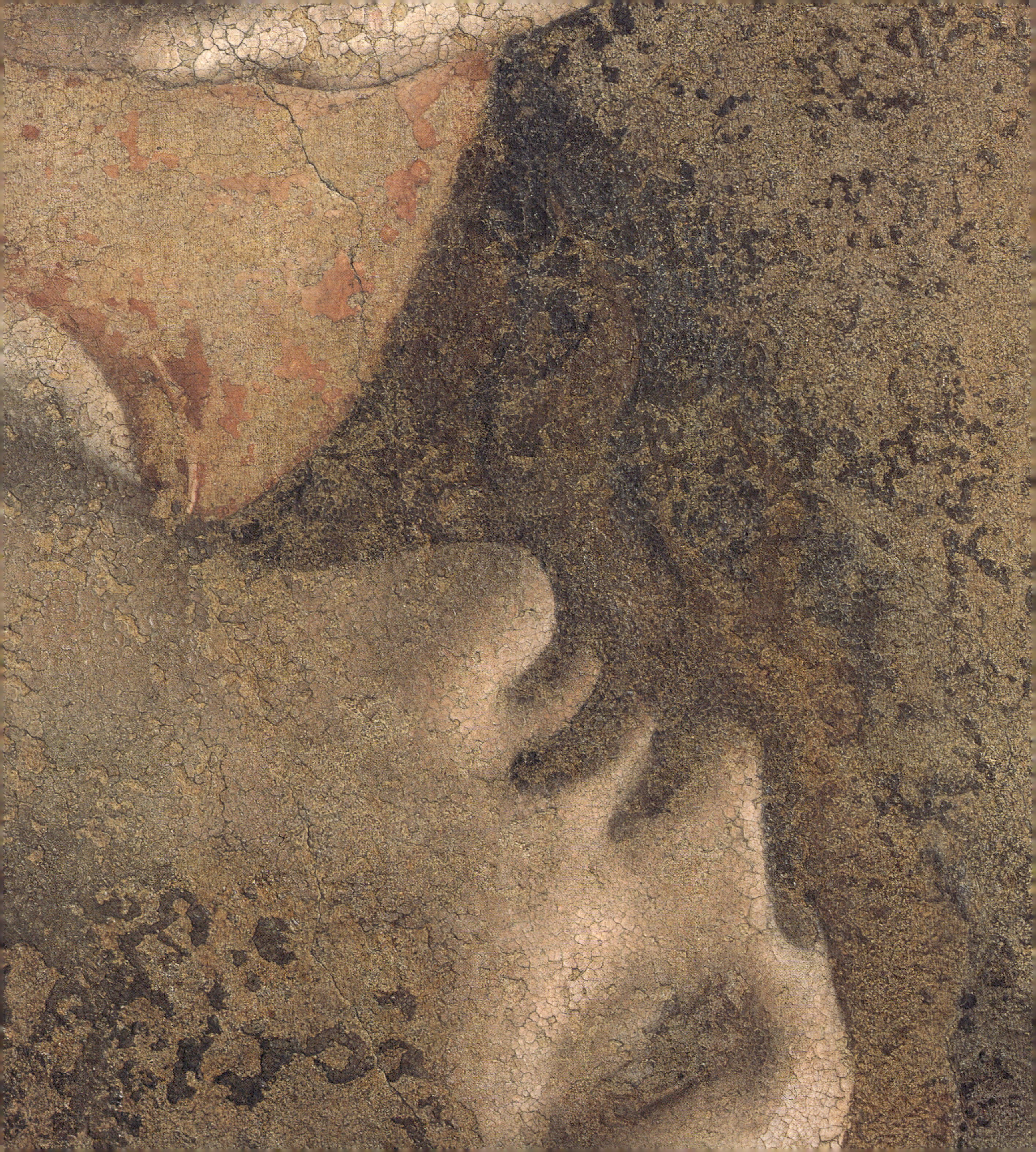

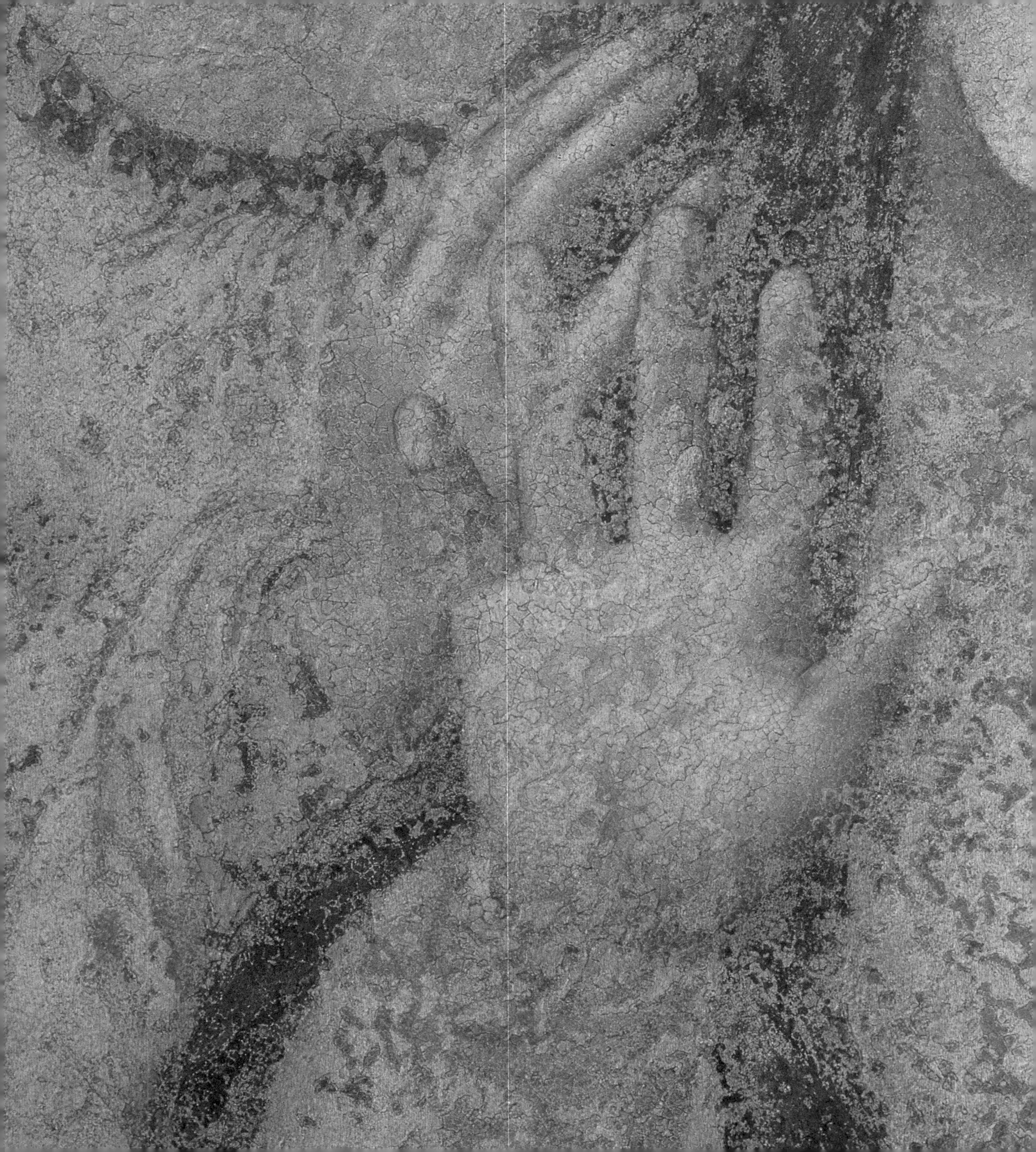

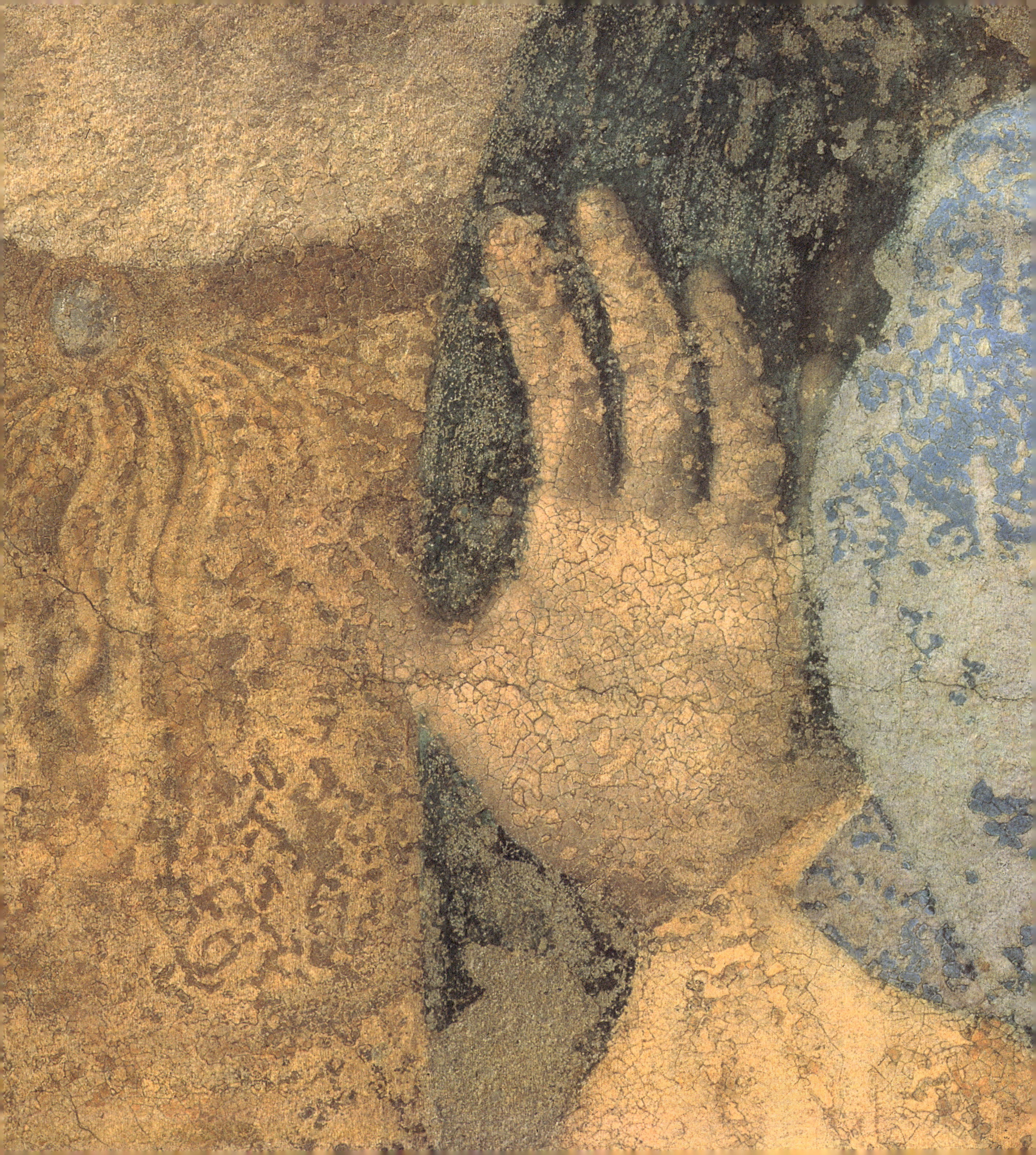

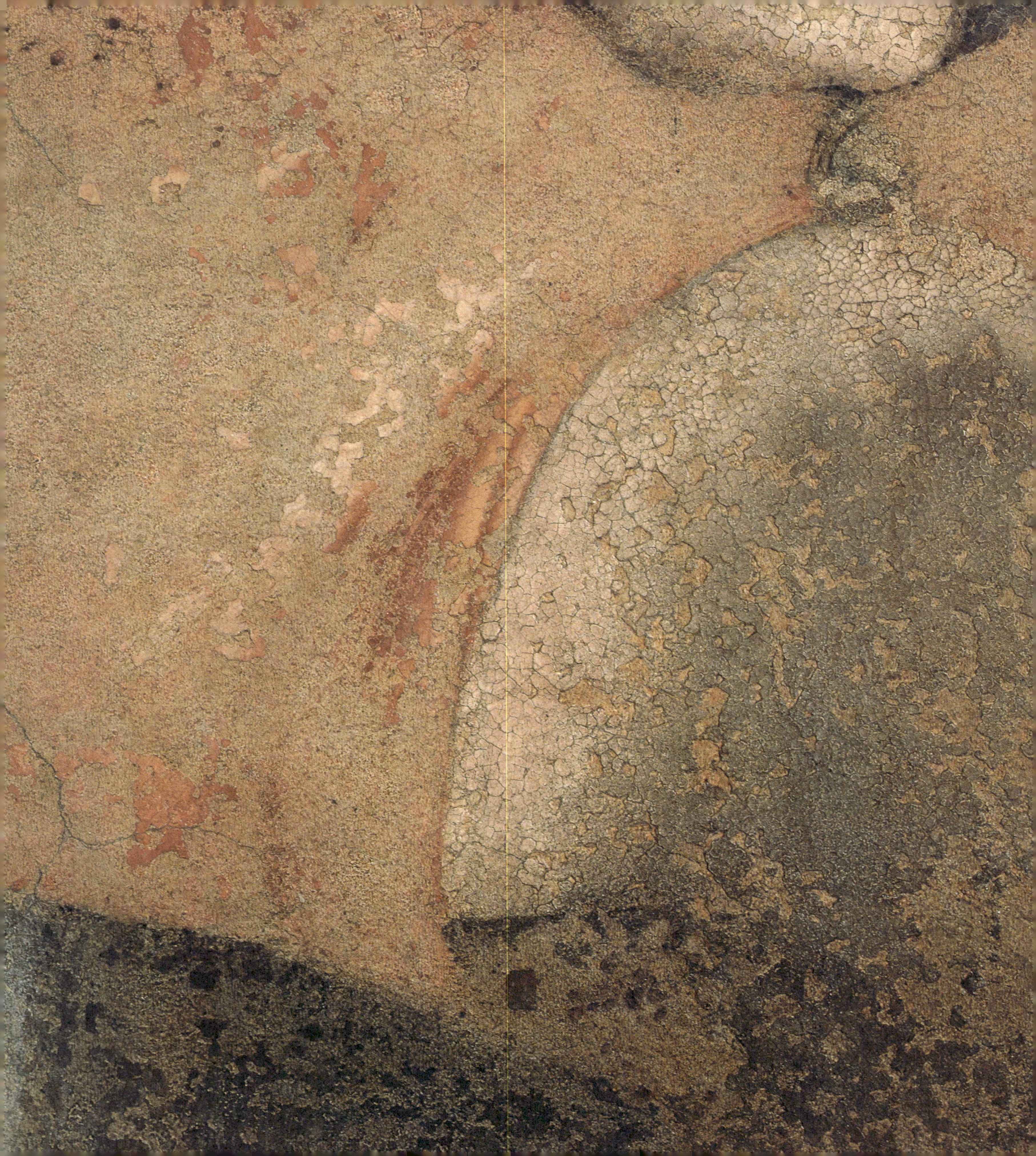

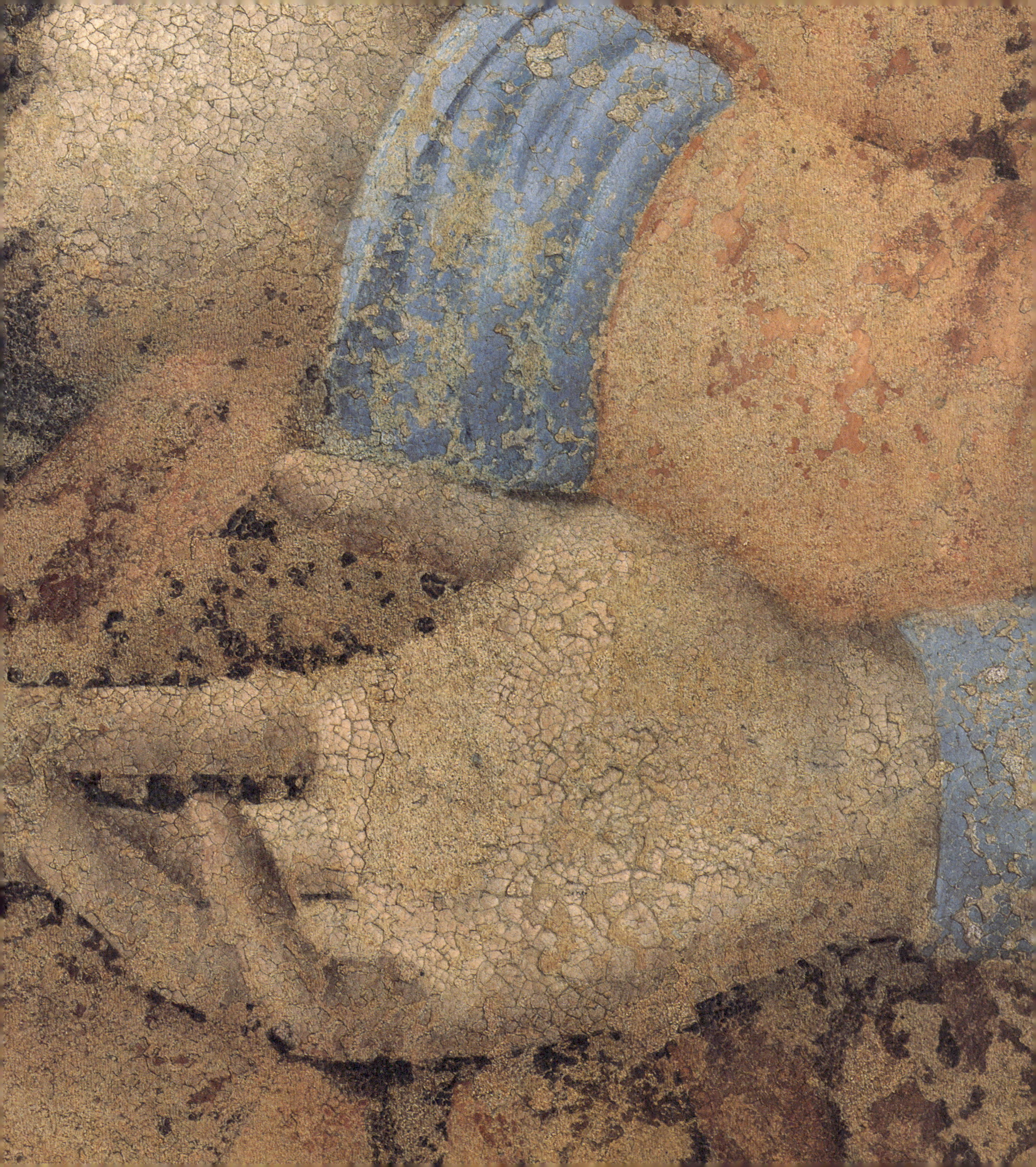

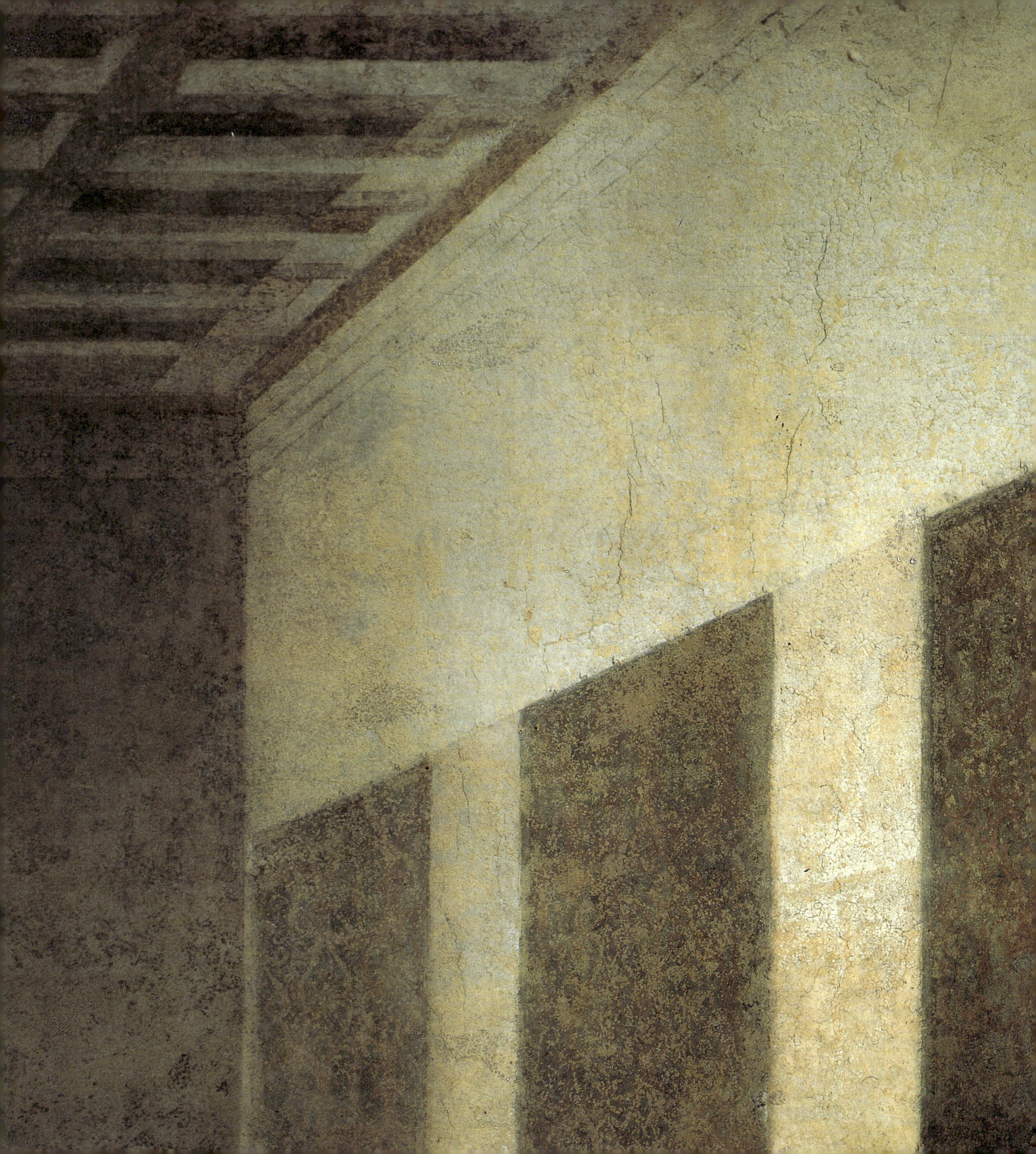

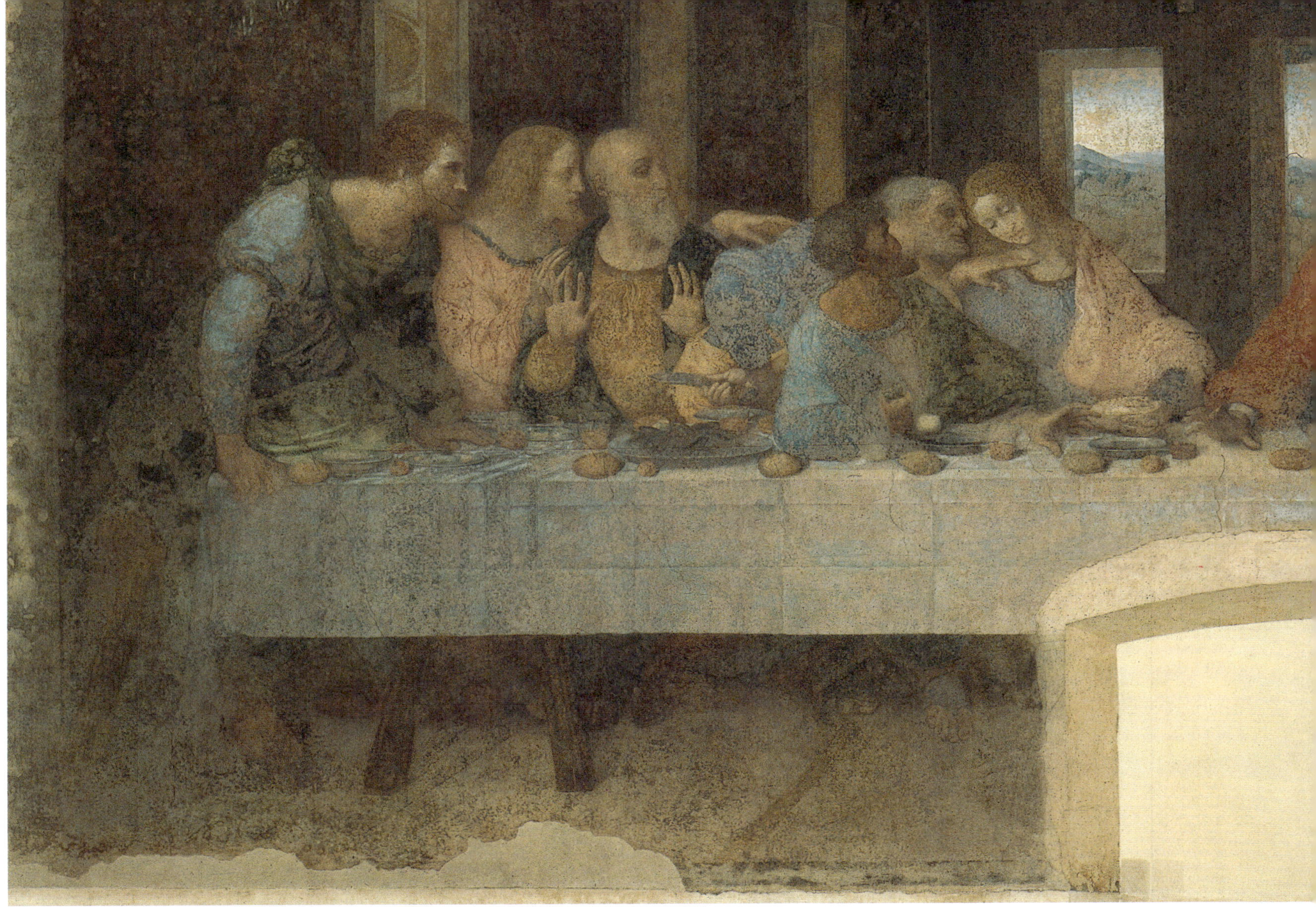

In the lunette at the top are heraldic devices and ornaments of the Sforza family

Bartholomew

James the Lesser

Andrew

Judas

Peter

John

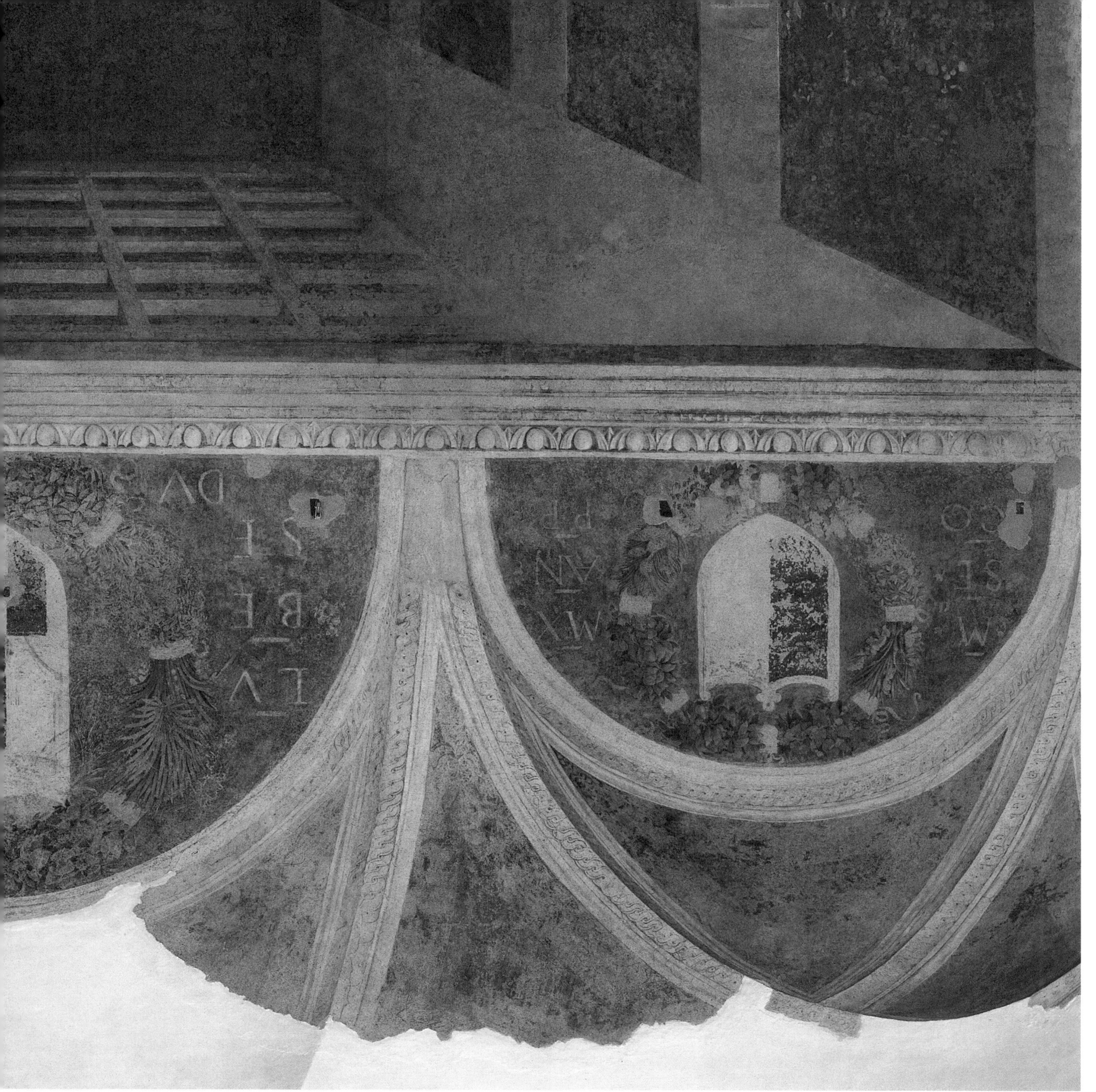

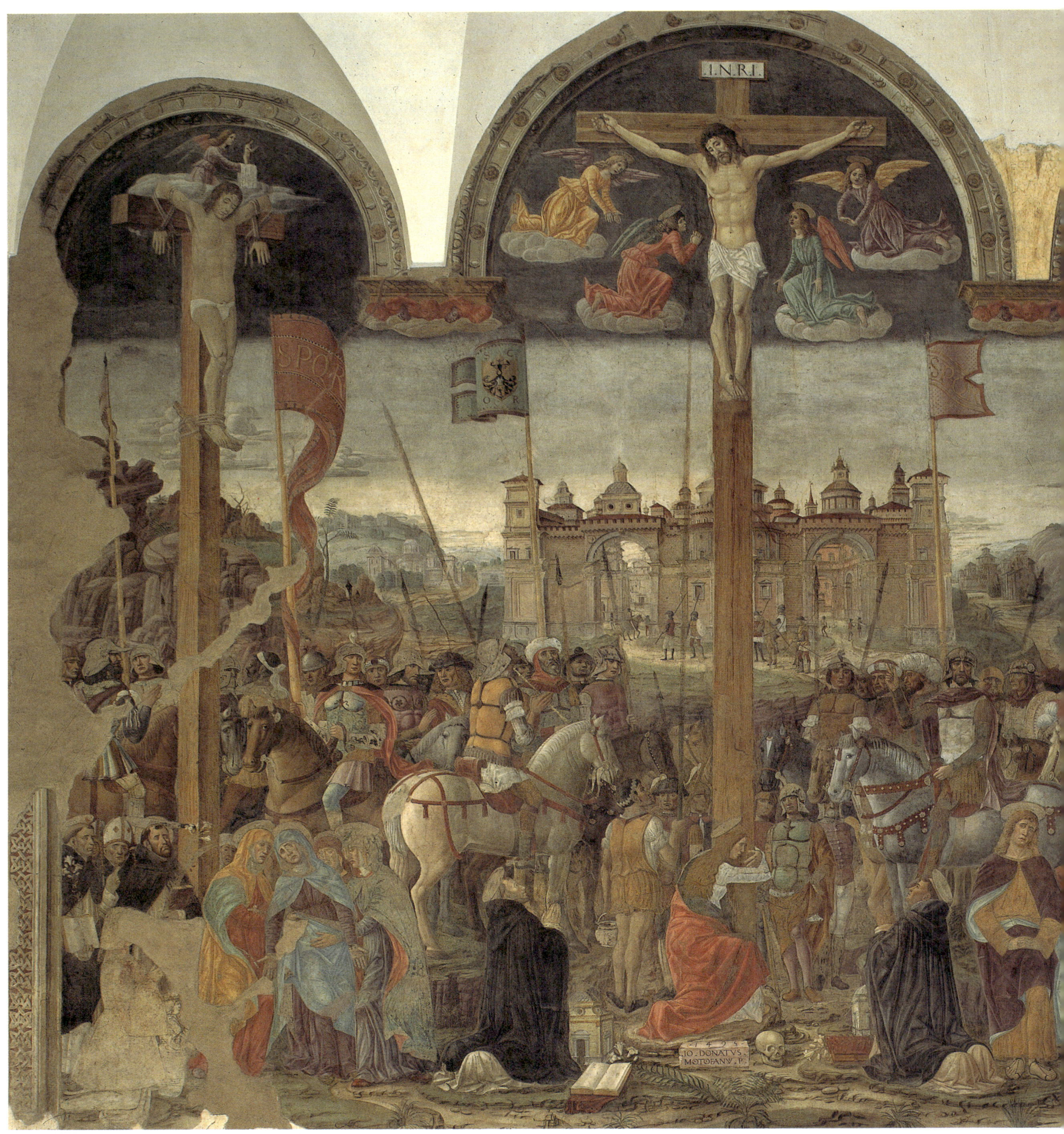

I.N.R.I.
SPQR
·1495·
IO. DONATVS.
MOTOFANV. P.

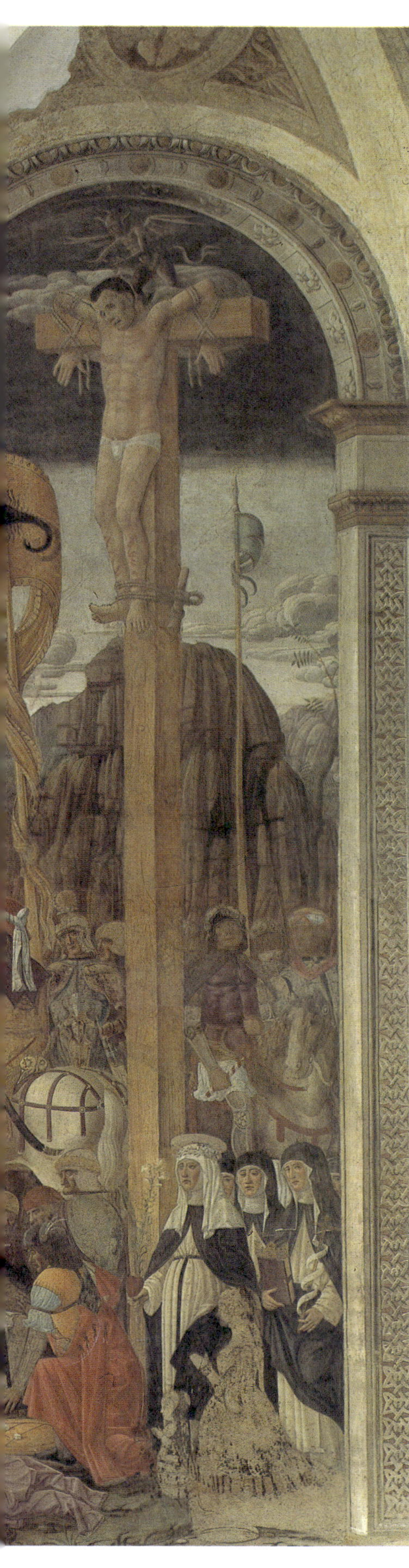

Donato da Montorfano, *Crucifixion*, 1495, south wall of the refectory. The portraits of the family of Ludovico il Moro at the ends of the fresco, now almost completely faded, are the work of Leonardo.

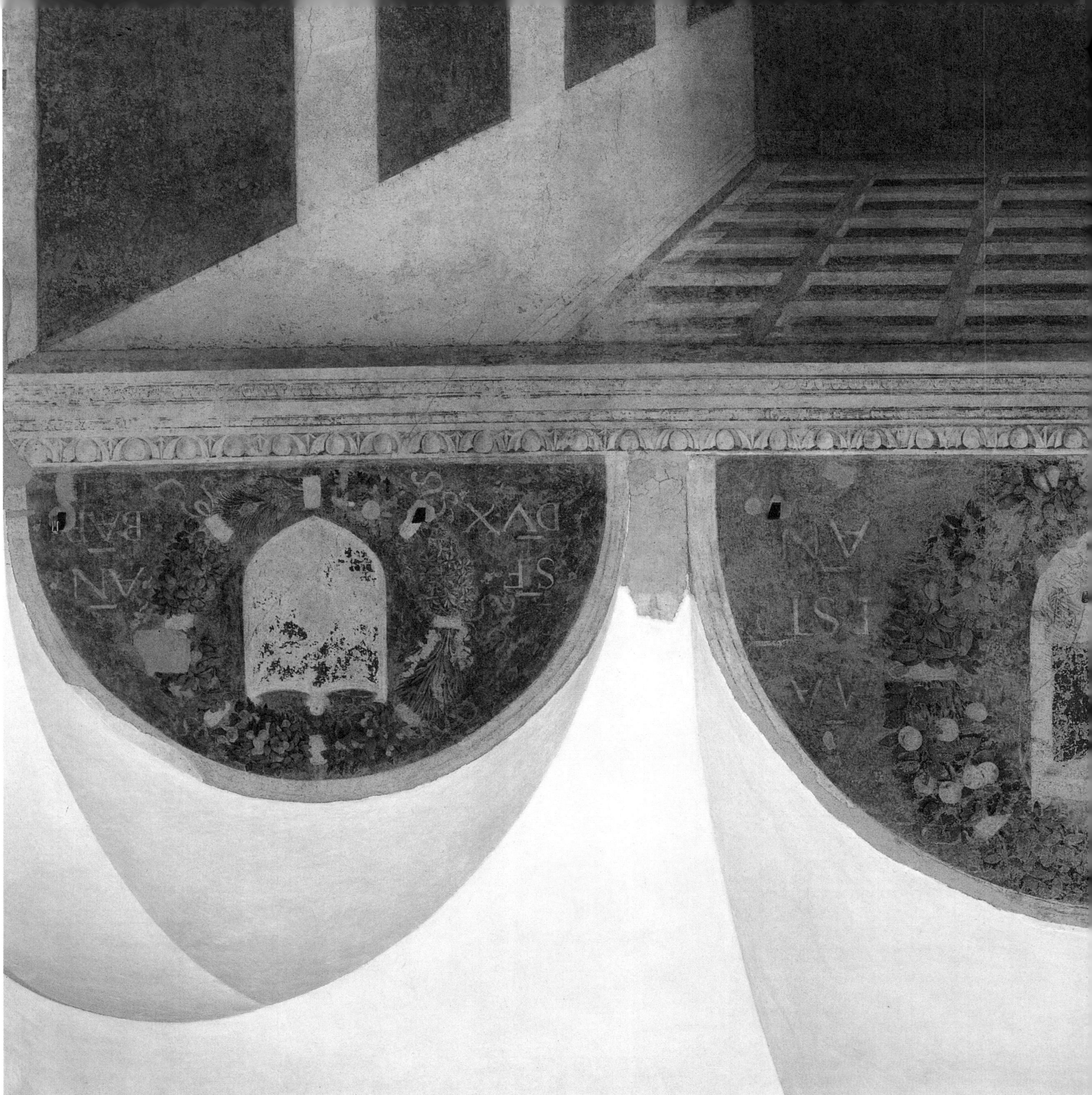

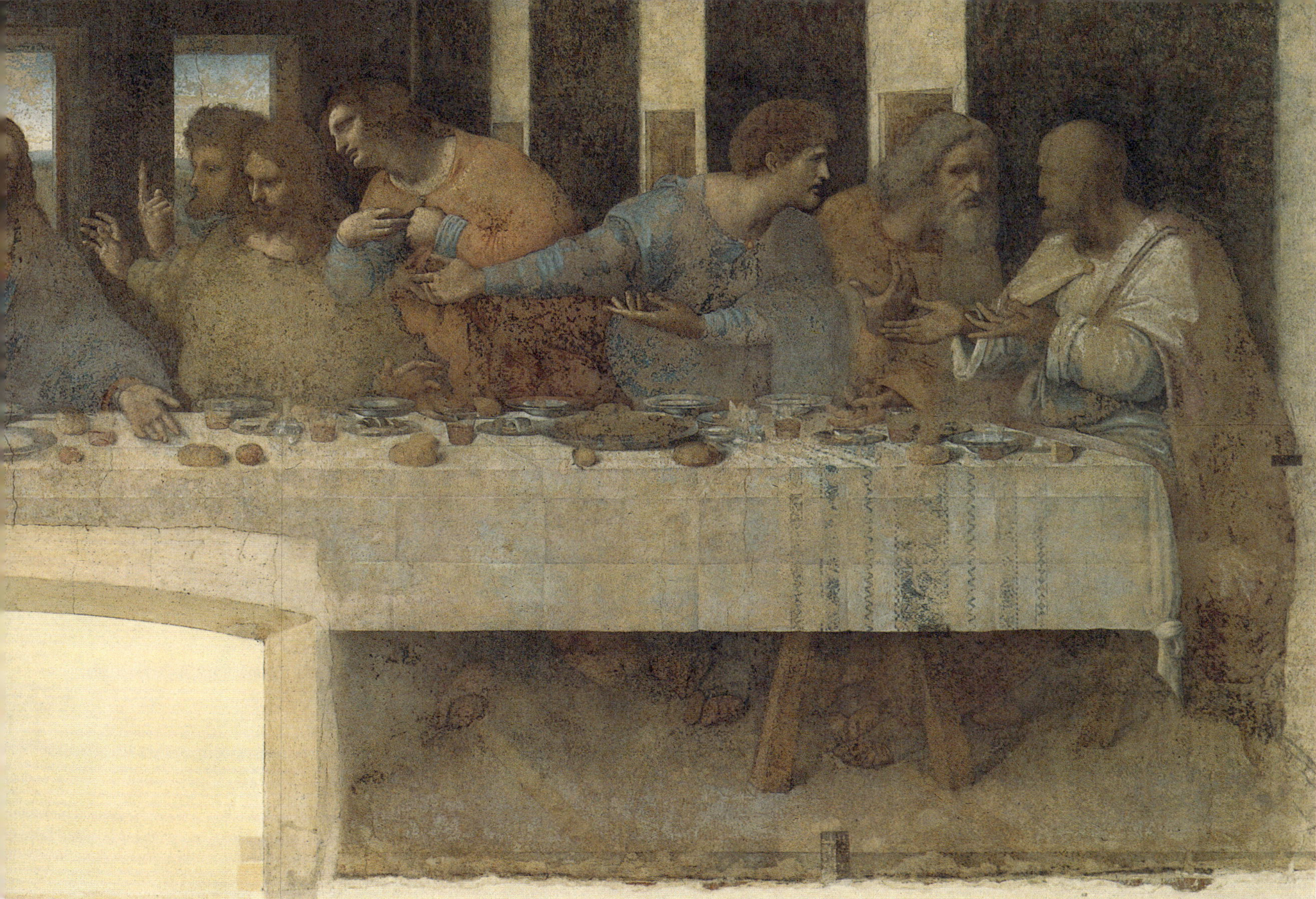

rist | Thomas | James the Greater | Philip | Matthew | Jude (Thaddaeus) | Simon

Leonardo da Vinci
The Last Supper

edited by
Vito Zani

English Translation
Christopher Huw Evans

Photographic credits

Antonio Quattrone, Florence

The images have been reproduced by permission of the Ministry of Cultural Assets and Activities

First published in the United States of America in 2001 by
Rizzoli International Publications, Inc.
300 Park Avenue South
New York, NY 10010

ISBN 0-8478-2352-0
LC 00-106611

Printed and bound in Italy

Octavius
Registered trademark, model and concept
Gallimard-Zanardi